SECOND EDITION

BRIDGING
Learning

This book is dedicated to professor Reuven Feuerstein, whose belief system, theory of cognition and cognitive modifiability, insight into cognitive dysfunction, and thinking skills program constitute the inspiration and mainspring of our work. We are thankful for his continued support of our efforts in the interpretation and applications of his ideas and concepts in this publication.

SECOND EDITION

BRIDGING
Learning

Unlocking Cognitive
Potential In and Out
of the Classroom

Mandia Mentis

Marilyn Dunn-Bernstein

Marténe Mentis

Mervyn Skuy

CORWIN
A SAGE Company

For information:

Corwin
A SAGE Company
2455 Teller Road
Thousand Oaks, California 91320
(800) 233-9936
Fax: (800) 417-2466
www.corwinpress.com

SAGE Ltd.
1 Oliver's Yard
55 City Road
London EC1Y 1SP
United Kingdom

SAGE India Pvt. Ltd.
B 1/I 1 Mohan Cooperative Industrial Area
Mathura Road, New Delhi 110 044
India

SAGE Asia-Pacific Pte. Ltd.
33 Pekin Street #02-01
Far East Square
Singapore 048763

Printed in the United States of America.

Library of Congress Cataloging-in-Publication Data

Bridging learning : unlocking cognitive potential in and out of the classroom/Mandia Mentis . . . [et al.].—2nd ed.
      p. cm.
Includes bibliographical references and index.
ISBN 978-1-4129-6994-9 (cloth)
ISBN 978-1-4129-6995-6 (pbk.)
   1. Thought and thinking—Study and teaching. 2. Cognition in children. 3. Cognitive learning.
I. Mentis, M. T. II. Title.

LB1590.3.B73 2009
370.15′2—dc22   2009000047

This book is printed on acid-free paper.

09 10 11 12 13   10 9 8 7 6 5 4 3 2 1

Acquisitions Editor:	Cathy Hernandez
Editorial Assistant:	Sarah Bartlett
Production Editor:	Cassandra Margaret Seibel
Copy Editor:	Adam Dunham
Typesetter:	C&M Digitals (P) Ltd.
Proofreader:	Jennifer Gritt
Cover Designer:	Karine Hovsepian

Contents

Preface

Bridging Learning—Thinking Skills to Unlock Cognitive Potential has been specifically designed for use by all educators—teachers, parents, community workers, and counselors. It is aimed at providing illustrations and applications of 14 key thinking skills that can be applied to multiple environments. The book is based on Reuven Feuerstein's (1980) Instrumental Enrichment (IE) thinking skills program. Feuerstein's theories and programs have made a significant contribution to developments in cognitive psychology, which have resulted in the burgeoning field of cognitive education—now an integral part of many education systems.

The aim of cognitive education is to develop thinking skills, enhance adaptive behavior, and promote effective functioning and self-realization. Cognitive education stresses individual and social modifiability as well as intellectual awareness and enrichment. Recognition that cognitive development in general, and thinking skills in particular, should be central to the educational process, has resulted in the development of various programs to enhance thinking. Feuerstein's IE program is a prototype of such programs and focuses on 14 specific thinking skills and their applications.

Bridging Learning—Thinking Skills to Unlock Cognitive Potential outlines these 14 thinking skills in the IE program and provides a wide variety of examples and activities to illustrate their application. These activities link the thinking skills to the conventional school curriculum as well as to nonformal and informal educational settings. The illustrations show how the thinking skills address global issues and problems facing all countries and cultures. They promote creative thinking, emotional development, and cross-cultural awareness.

This book is not intended as a substitute for the IE program, but as a companion volume to it, and it offers bridging examples for each of the thinking skills. The concept of bridging is central to Feuerstein's theory and refers to the ability to transcend an experience in one aspect of life and apply it in other spheres. Bridging involves formulating principles and rules, and then testing and applying these rules and principles in a variety of situations, which in turn leads to modifying and formulating further principles.

Bridging Learning—Thinking Skills to Unlock Cognitive Potential is also intended to enhance the cognitive repertoire of the educator. It demonstrates the wide range of areas where the thinking skills, principles, and strategies contained within the IE program can be applied in the classroom, home, and community. These are not meant as a definitive or exhaustive list of areas or activities. It is essential that, in the spirit of creativity and interaction between mediator and learner, original bridging activities are generated. Thus, the activities in this book provide examples of how creative teachers can further bridge the 14 thinking skills.

Since the publication of the first edition of this book in 1999, research and training in IE and cognitive education has continued to flourish. The IE program has been translated into more than 20 languages, and been applied in more than 45 countries, in diverse cultural contexts, and on virtually all of the continents of the globe. This diversity of IE is also evident through its use in regular schools and in programs for students with special learning needs, at colleges and universities, in business and industrial settings, in clinical rehabilitation settings and prisons, and in populations of the elderly.

The first edition of this book was a product of the Cognitive Research Programme (CRP) of the University of the Witwatersrand (1989–2004). The CRP developed and applied aspects of the IE program in a variety of settings, including teachers' colleges, schools, and community centers, and results of these research projects have been published and presented internationally. The current authors developed the original edition of this publication along with *Mediated Learning—Teaching, Tasks, and Tools to unlock Cognitive Potential,* which is also now published as a second edition by Corwin. Both these publications serve as companion publications to Feuerstein's IE and mediated learning experience (MLE) programs.

Bridging Learning—Thinking Skills to Unlock Cognitive Potential is an invaluable resource for all those involved in education. It provides extensive application of the 14 thinking skills, as well as critical coverage of Feuerstein's theory of cognitive enrichment and its international applications. The publication serves as a useful reference on cognitive education, as well as an excellent practical guide to mediating thinking skills for teachers, parents, community workers, and counselors.

Acknowledgments

Corwin gratefully acknowledges the contributions of the following reviewers:

Yolanda Abel
Instructor, Teacher Preparation
Johns Hopkins University
Baltimore, MD

Carole Basile
Associate Dean and Associate Professor, Teacher Education
University of Colorado
Denver, CO

Shelia Duncan
Spanish Teacher
Boyd County High School
Ashland, KY

John Forsyth
Journalism Teacher
Waynesville High School
Waynesville, MO

Pam Jackson
Seventh-Grade Teacher
Elkhorn Middle School
Frankfort, KY

Betty Brandenburg Yundt
Sixth-Grade Teacher and Curriculum Coordinator, Grades 4–6
Walker Intermediate School
Fort Knox, KY

About the Authors

Mandia Mentis is an educational psychologist and senior lecturer in the special education and educational psychology program at Massey University, New Zealand. She is an accredited trainer of Feuerstein's Instrumental Enrichment (FIE) and the Learning Potential Assessment Device (LPAD), having completed her training at the International Centre for Learning Enhancement in Israel under Professor Feuerstein. Over the past 30 years, she has run Feuerstein Instrumental Enrichment (FIE) workshops with the Cognitive Research Centre in South Africa and with the Australasian Institute for Learning Enhancement in New Zealand. She has contributed extensively to research projects and publications and has cowritten and published two books on mediated learning and Instrumental Enrichment. She has taught at primary, secondary, and tertiary levels and has worked as an educational psychologist in both special- and inclusive-education settings. Her teaching and research interests include cognitive assessment, teaching for diversity, and e-learning. Her doctoral research focused on developing online communities of practice in special education and educational psychology teaching programs.

Marilyn Dunn-Bernstein is an eminent educator with nearly 40 years experience in all types of educational environments. She holds a PhD in education, a master's degree in psychology and a degree in human behavior. With both a research and practical background, she has studied under Reuven Feuerstein and implemented the principles of structural cognitive modifiability, IE, and MLE in an extensive range of educational settings. These include 10 years of research, lecturing and publishing with the Cognitive Research Unit of the University of the Witwatersrand, and 16 years of work with the Gifted Child Program for disadvantaged individuals in South African townships. Her current work as a psychologist in Australia involves enhancing cognitive, emotional, and creative development in Autistic, Down syndrome, Asperger's, and gifted individuals. She also works with psychology and social sciences students, is an external examiner for the Institute of Counseling, and has been part of the team that runs Feuerstein workshops in Australia, New Zealand, and South Africa.

Marténe Mentis is an independent scholar, artist, and illustrator currently teaching fulltime at Hato Petera College in Auckland, New Zealand. She has 20 years experience in education and has taught at primary, secondary, and tertiary levels. Her diverse educational background includes 6 years with the Cognitive Research Centre, University of the Witwatersrand, South Africa, where she contributed to research, lectured in FIE workshops, and helped develop educational resources, including two books on mediated learning and Instrumental Enrichment. She completed her training in FIE under Professor Feuerstein at the International Centre for Learning Enhancement in Israel, and in LPAD at the Cognitive Research Centre in South Africa. She has an honors degree in fine arts and a master's degree in education.

 **Mervyn Skuy** is a clinical and educational psychologist who has worked for many years in researching and teaching Feuerstein's theories and approaches. From 1985 to 2003 he did this within the framework of the Cognitive Research Programme, which he established and directed at the University of the Witwatersrand in South Africa. During this time, he was also professor and head of the division of specialized education at that university. He was professor of educational psychology and specialized education at Touro College in New York, and has taught courses in Instrumental Enrichment and mediated learning experience to various organizations and target groups in South Africa, the United States, Israel, Canada, and France. His research has been published in American, British, Canadian, Australian, Dutch, and South African journals and books. He is currently professor emeritus at the University of the Witwatersrand and in private practice as a psychologist. He is also a consultant to Feuerstein's International Centre for the Enhancement of Learning Potential (ICELP). In this capacity, he is actively engaged in teaching Instrumental Enrichment and in developing programs of study within a project that the ICELP has established in South Africa.

Introduction

Putting Feuerstein's IE Program Into Practice

> *What are the building blocks of efficient thinking? How can teachers use subject teaching to promote cognitive development? How can parents or caretakers teach children thinking skills within the home? How can thinking skills promote interpersonal development, enhance creativity, and facilitate multicultural awareness?*

This book attempts to answer these questions by bridging 14 thinking skills from Feuerstein's (1980) Instrumental Enrichment (IE) program to both formal and informal learning settings. Feuerstein's theory behind IE is initially outlined in this introduction to provide a framework for discussing each of the 14 cognitive operations. These 14 thinking skills are then described in the subsequent chapters of this book, and examples are provided of bridging these thinking skills to a range of different contexts.

WHO IS FEUERSTEIN AND WHAT IS HIS COGNITIVE THEORY?

Reuven Feuerstein is an internationally renowned Israeli professor of psychology and a scholar in the field of child development. Through his work with individuals who are low functioning and disadvantaged, he developed innovative methods of testing and teaching. In common with other contemporary psychologists, he rejected the notion that people are born with a certain intelligence that remains fixed and static throughout life. In contrast, he proposed that learning occurs through ongoing interaction with others within a social context and that it is this interaction that facilitates change and modifiability in our cognitive processes.

Feuerstein developed his theory around this learning interaction that he called *mediated learning experience* (MLE). He believed that through MLE the learner develops efficient thinking skills that he described as the *cognitive functions.* Efficient cognitive functions can be developed through manipulating the learning task—which Feuerstein refers to as the *cognitive map.* These three aspects of his theory—mediated learning experience, cognitive functions, and the cognitive map—form the operational tools or techniques that can be used to ensure that cognitive modifiability, or change in the learner, occurs. These concepts can be illustrated in the form of a triangle—where at the heart of the triangle lies the belief that all people are modifiability or open to change (structural cognitive modifiability). Change or modifiability can occur through using the three techniques of MLE, cognitive functions, and cognitive tasks. This can be illustrated in the diagram of the Feuerstein triangle where each of the three points of the triangle relate to the triad of the learning process—the teacher, the learner, and the task. The teacher guides the learning interaction through using the criteria of MLE in interacting with the learner. Through this interaction, change occurs in the learner's cognitive functions. The mediated interaction and changes in thinking relate to analyzing and adjusting the learning task using the cognitive map.

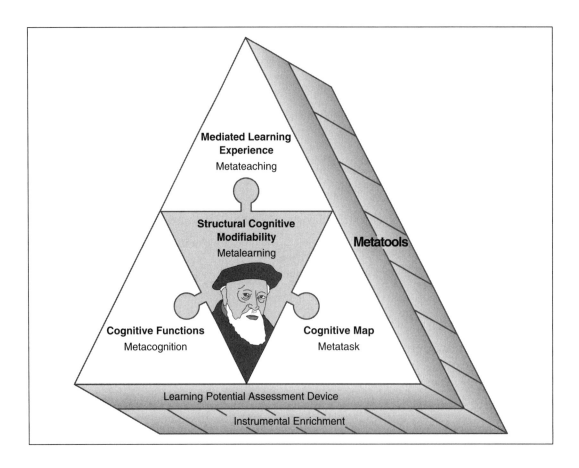

Note: These concepts are explored in depth in *Mediated Learning—Teaching, Tasks, and Tools to Unlock Cognitive Potential,* Second Edition, published by Corwin, and which is the sister publication to this book. In addition, these are detailed in the appendixes, which provide the full list of the criteria of MLE (Appendix A), the cognitive functions (Appendix B), and the cognitive map (Appendix C).

As illustrated in the diagram above, the core of the Feuerstein triangle is the theory of structural cognitive modifiability—the belief that all individuals have the potential to change and learn. This change occurs during an MLE focusing on the thinking skills (cognitive functions) of the learner and adjusting the learning task using the cognitive map.

MLE consists of 12 criteria describing the learning interaction. These are outlined in detail in Appendix A. The three essential elements of MLE are intentionality and reciprocity (focused learning), meaning (purposeful learning), and transcendence (bridging learning). Mediating these three criteria in any learning interaction are necessary to promote the development of critical thinking skills. The remaining 9 criteria are used in different ways in different contexts to enhance learning. Examples of these are provided within the bridging illustrations in the following chapters. Using MLE in the learning interaction involves thinking about teaching or *metateaching.*

The cognitive functions are grouped according to three phases of thinking—the input (taking in stimuli), elaboration (thinking through the problem), and output (communicating a response) phases. These are presented in table form in Appendix B. The list of cognitive functions provides useful descriptors of thinking and can be used to better understand and help the learner who might experience difficulties with a task. Examples of these are provided within the bridging illustrations in the following chapters. Thinking about thinking involves *metacognition.*

The cognitive map is a tool used to assess a task or leaning experience and break it down into component parts in order to assess where a learner might be experiencing difficulty. It provides four layers of analysis: the content or subject matter of the task; the modality or language of presentation of the task; the level of abstraction, novelty, and complexity of the task; and the cognitive operations required by the task. The cognitive map is explained in Appendix C. It is a useful tool for analyzing a task and then, by altering the layers, providing different and alternative approaches to solving the task for the learner. Manipulating the dimensions of a task provides multiple ways to approach the learning experience. Examples of these are provided within the bridging illustrations in the following chapters. Thinking about how to adapt the learning experience involves a *metatask* analysis.

The goal of the Feuerstein approach is to facilitate autonomous and independent learning. This goal can be achieved, according to Feuerstein, by using the three techniques illustrated in the triangle. Structural cognitive modifiability (or change) is achieved by using the criteria of MLE to re-mediate cognitive functions through adapting the task using the cognitive map. Thus by using the right task with the right kind of interaction, cognitive development and change can occur for the learner.

These techniques form the basis of the Feuerstein approach on which his two programs (*metatools*) are based. The first program is an assessment package developed by Feuerstein called the Learning Potential Assessment Device (LPAD). This program provides dynamic assessment of an individual's potential to learn through MLE. The second program developed by Feuerstein is the thinking skills program of Instrumental Enrichment (IE)—which is the subject of this book. The two programs can be conceptualized as being the products or applications of Feuerstein's theory. Both of these programs have as their core the belief in structural cognitive modifiability. Both programs rely on MLE to develop the cognitive functions of the learner through manipulating the task using the cognitive map. The link between these two programs to the theory can be illustrated as in the diagram above, where the theory and techniques form the Feuerstein triangle, and the programs are the products that align with these.

WHAT IS IE?

Feuerstein's IE program makes use of pencil-and-paper exercises to develop thinking skills. The IE program consists of 14 instruments that introduce the different thinking skills or cognitive operations. The "instruments" are tools that provide enrichment in thinking in the 14 areas. In this book, each of these thinking skills is described and then bridged or applied to both formal and informal learning context. Links to research using IE are described throughout each of the chapters.

What are others saying about IE?

"Instrumental Enrichment is most simply described as a strategy for learning to learn. It uses abstract, content-free, organizational, spatial, temporal and perceptual exercises that involve a wide range of mental operations and thought processes. The aim of the Feuerstein Instrumental Enrichment (FIE) program is to change the overall cognitive structure of the (impaired) performer by transforming his passive and dependent cognitive style into that characteristic of an autonomous and independent thinker." (Feuerstein & Jensen, 1980, p. 401)

"The overall aim of the Instrumental Enrichment exercises is to turn children with a reduced ability to be modified—to learn and adapt—into much more flexible and reflective operators in the world. By changing and enriching a child's structure of thinking, Instrumental Enrichment makes him/her more receptive to stimuli and experience, and increasingly able to cope with new conditions and situations confronting him/her in life and, of course, in school." (Sharron, 1987, p. 96)

Children's reactions to IE:

"It's brilliant for your brains."
"It helps you not to be impulsive—before I used to rush into things."
"It helped me not to be frightened of new things."
"It helped me to think."
"It helped me do my other lessons."

(Sharron, 1987, p. 95)

Teacher's reactions to IE:

"It gives me insight into the process underlying students' thinking."
"It shows how to ask questions and accept there is more than one answer."
"More of this enrichment is needed."
"It should be introduced at High School."
"I have found different and alternative ways of looking at and doing things . . ."
"It has helped me try more approaches to problems, rather than just focusing on answers."

(Skuy, Lomofsky, Green, & Fridjhon, 1993, p. 92)

THE AIM OF THIS BOOK

The aim of *Bridging Learning—Thinking Skills to Unlock Cognitive Potential* is to elaborate and bridge the thinking skills presented in Feuerstein's Instrumental Enrichment (IE) program. This book is a companion to Feuerstein's IE program, providing an explanation of what each of the 14 thinking skills are, why they are important, and when and where they could be used. The book then offers suggestions for transcending these thinking skills into both formal and informal learning areas. Bridging the thinking skills into formal settings includes examples of classroom situations and specific subject content, to show how school experiences can be used to mediate thinking skills. In informal learning areas, examples are given where everyday activities in the home and community situations can be used to teach thinking skills to promote interpersonal development, enhance creativity, and facilitate multicultural awareness.

THE FORMAT OF THIS BOOK

The format for all 14 chapters of *Bridging Learning—Thinking Skills to Unlock Cognitive Potential* is the same. Each chapter deals with one thinking skill/cognitive operation. The outline for each chapter is as follows:

> An introduction to the thinking skill, linking to the Feuerstein IE instrument and explaining the logo or symbol for the IE instrument.

> A description of the thinking skill, noting *what* it is, *why* it is important, and *when* and *where* it is used.

> A cognitive conundrum that provides a controversial comment or counter argument relating to the instrument.

> A list of examples that bridge the thinking skill to *formal learning contexts* with examples from the school setting and curriculum.

> A list of examples that bridge the thinking skill to *informal learning contexts* with examples from the home, community, or counseling contexts.

> An example in practice showing application to a range of contexts including the home, school, or community.

> An outline of how the thinking skill is integrated with Feuerstein's theory of *mediated learning experience*, the *cognitive functions*, and the *cognitive map*.

> A window to *International Research on Cognitive Education* where examples are provided from the literature outlining research projects using IE in a variety of contexts, countries, and with different population groups.

> Final quotations are presented for an overall metacognitive reflection on each chapter.

Thinking Skill	*Feuerstein's Instrument*
Organization Chapter 1 covers Feuerstein's instrument of ORGANIZATION OF DOTS, which involves creating order out of discrete and unconnected items by linking, structuring, and connecting items.	
Comparisons Chapter 2 covers Feuerstein's instrument of COMPARISON, which involves finding similarities and differences between items according to relevant and appropriate criteria.	
Categorization Chapter 3 covers Feuerstein's instrument of CATEGORIZATION, which involves grouping elements according to appropriate principals and placing items into particular classes or groups.	
Relational Orientation in Space Chapter 4 covers Feuerstein's instrument of ORIENTATION IN SPACE I, which involves understanding that one's relative position in space depends on an internal reference system—the direction that one is facing.	
Cardinal Orientation in Space Chapter 5 covers Feuerstein's instrument of ORIENTATION IN SPACE II, which uses the cardinal points of the compass—North, South, East, and West—as the reference system to orient oneself in space.	
Analysis and Synthesis Chapter 6 covers Feuerstein's instrument of ANALYTIC PERCEPTION, which involves the skill of breaking a whole into its parts and putting the parts together to make a whole.	
Problem Solving Chapter 7 covers Feuerstein's instrument of ILLUSTRATIONS, which involves identifying that something has gone wrong (disequilibrium), analyzing why it has gone wrong, and finding solutions to make it right (restoring equilibrium to a system).	

Thinking Skill	*Feuerstein's Instrument*
Relationships Chapter 8 covers Feuerstein's instrument of FAMILY RELATIONS, which focuses on inferring, understanding, and explaining the connection between two or more people or groups and their involvement with each other.	
Temporal Concepts Chapter 9 covers Feuerstein's instrument of TEMPORAL RELATIONS, which involves having an understanding of the concept of time.	
Instructions Chapter 10 covers Feuerstein's instrument of INSTRUCTIONS, which relate to the two reciprocal processes of encoding (giving) and decoding (receiving) information.	
Progressions Chapter 11 covers Feuerstein's instrument of NUMERICAL PROGRESSIONS, which focuses on identifying rules that govern the repeated patterns that occur between events.	
Transitive Relations Chapter 12 covers Feuerstein's instrument of TRANSITIVE RELATIONS, which focuses on transferring information from two pairs of items to a third pair.	
Syllogisms Chapter 13 covers Feuerstein's instrument of SYLLOGISMS, which focuses on syllogistic reasoning, where from two given premises that have a common middle term, a third premise—called the conclusion—is deduced.	
Scaffolding Chapter 14 covers Feuerstein's instrument of REPRESENTATIONAL STENCIL DESIGN, which focuses on the cognitive operations involved in mentally reconstructing an event or outcome by looking at the end product.	

Source: Adapted from Feuerstein, R., & Jensen, M. (1980). Instrumental enrichment: Theoretical basis, goals and instruments. *Educational Forum* 44(4), 401–423.

1

Organization

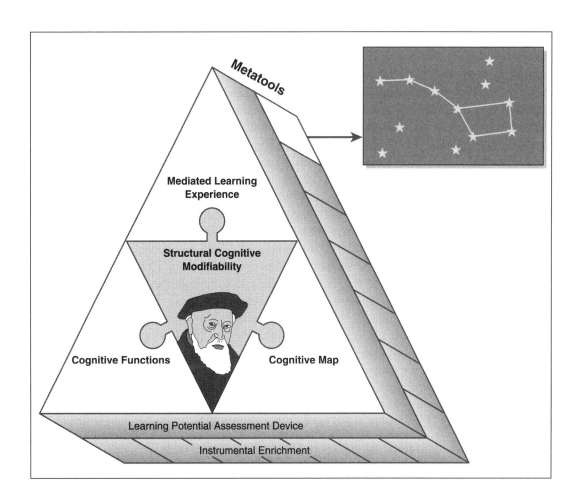

The thinking skill that is outlined in this chapter is *organization*. Organization involves creating order out of discrete and unconnected items. Order is imposed by linking, structuring, and organizing items. For example, a group of seemingly unrelated people can be linked through different forms of relationships—family members, friends, work colleagues, and so on.

The thinking skill of organization is taught in the *organization of dots instrument* of Feuerstein's (1980) Instrumental Enrichment (IE) program. Feuerstein's symbol for the organization of dots instrument is the Big Dipper, a constellation of stars found in the northern hemisphere. In the Big Dipper symbol, imaginary lines connect a group of stars into a recognizable and distinguishable pattern. Linking items together into a pattern illustrates the cognitive operation of organization.

ORGANIZATION—WHAT, WHY, WHEN, AND WHERE?

Why is the dictionary organized from A to Z? How are books ordered in a library?

In what section of the supermarket would you look for the milk?

How are calendars and timetables structured?

The ability to answer these kinds of questions depends on the thinking skill of organization. We are born into a world of stimuli that are seemingly unrelated and disconnected. Order is imposed on these stimuli through linking objects and events according to relationships and rules. This is the process of organization. Different cultures, societies, or groups organize events, activities, objects, and stimuli in different ways depending on the mores and practices of that culture or context. Organization gives meaning and purpose to the world.

Without organization we would have what Feuerstein (1980) calls an *episodic grasp of reality*. In episodic reality, the world is perceived as consisting of separate, isolated, and unrelated episodes, events, or items. This perception of reality, where there is no organization, can result in confusion and chaos. In order to overcome the chaos and confusion of episodic reality, the skill of organizing is mediated. This varies depending on different contexts and cultures. For example, calendar months and years are organized in different ways according to different religions and festivals. Writing can be organized in a left to right, right to left, or top to bottom sequence depending on the language being written and the culture. Information can be organized in a sequential, linear, logical order as in the chapters of a book, or in a simultaneous, webbed, networked way as in a concept map or on the Internet. As the skill of organization is mediated, culture is transmitted. Thus, culture and context is mediated through the relationships that connect things and make order out of apparent chaos.

What Is the Thinking Skill of Organization?

Organization involves creating or recognizing the links and connections between objects and events and the rules, systems, or criteria that govern these connections. For example, words in a dictionary are organized according to an alphabetical ordering system. Air travel is organized according to scheduled times that flights depart and arrive. The general rule for sorting clothes for washing is into piles of whites, colors, darks, and delicates. Music and literature can be organized into genres, styles, or periods. School classes are organized according to the criteria of age and subject level.

Why Is the Thinking Skill of Organization Important?

There are many reasons for teaching the skill of organization. Organization aids understanding, creates order and meaning, and allows for efficiency and convenience. For example, an essay or assignment has greater clarity when it is organized into an introduction, body, and conclusion. Laws organized into a legal system provide a structure for people to understand their rights. Diaries or daily logs enable us to manage time more productively. Products in a discount or superstore organized into departments make it easier and quicker to find things such as groceries, kitchenware, gardening tools, and clothing.

When and Where Is the Thinking Skill of Organization Used?

There are numerous contexts and situations where organization occurs. Time can be organized into seconds, minutes, hours, days, weeks, seasons, years, centuries, and so on. Objects can be grouped according to different criteria—for example, food in a shop, books in a library, or clothes in a closet. Activities can be planned and arranged—for example, outings, parties, and tournaments and games have different organizational requirements. Ideas and thoughts can be organized in different ways—for example, poems, concept maps, overviews, and arguments all have different formal structures. Knowledge can be organized into different disciplines—for example science, fine arts, and humanities.

Cognitive Conundrum—Organization

There is a school of thought that suggests that parents and teachers, who constantly mediate organization to young children, actually inhibit their creative development. Statements such as "Put all your clothes on that shelf," "The green blocks go in that box," "Line up along this wall," and so on do not allow students freedom to explore their world of creative talents. Are we living in an overly organized world?

What do you think?

BRIDGING ORGANIZATION TO FORMAL LEARNING CONTEXTS

Numerous formal learning experiences can be used to mediate organization.

Humanities

- Become familiar with the way a dictionary is organized in order to use it more effectively and plan an essay or report using specific headings and subheadings.
- Mediate how language, grammar, and word structures are organized in terms of parts of speech, conjunctions, prefixes and suffixes, and so on.

Social Sciences

- Create timelines to illustrate the order of historical events.
- Use maps (such as political, physical, topical, or contour maps) to illustrate how land, people, and resources can be organized.

Sciences

- Examine how ecosystems are organized into food chains, life cycles, and so on.
- Discuss the organization and operation of body systems (e.g., the human respiratory system, digestive system, renal system).
- Organize statistical data by structuring it into pie graphs, line graphs, or bar graphs.
- Show how numerical values can be placed into columns for ease of computation (e.g., 10s, 100s, other units of measurement).

Arts

- Review how a poem, painting, piece of music, or art form is organized in order to aid its appreciation.
- Show how living spaces have been organized differently in various architectural periods.

Technology

- Examine the organization of Internet structures and show how they facilitate communication and research on a global scale.
- Select and study the workings of a manufacturing organization in terms of efficiencies of effort, labor usage, placing of machinery, safety measures, and so on.

BRIDGING ORGANIZATION TO INFORMAL LEARNING CONTEXTS

General

- Improve study skills. For example, apply organizational principles to structure a study timetable, a workplace, and the particular subject content in a mind map or overview.
- Develop a plan that can always be used to check or proofread written work.

Health and Personal Development

- Consider organization as a remedy for disorganization—disorganization can lead to negative emotions such as anger, frustration, and low self-esteem; and to feeling swamped and generally unable to cope.
- Work on ways to organize a day so that it reduces personal stress—for example, taking time out, doing meditation, following an interest or hobby, and so on.

Home

- Make a mundane shopping trip more meaningful by mediating to children how and why the products in a supermarket have been organized. For example, show how perishables are stored in refrigerated sections of the store and cleaning products are separated from food. Encourage children to use these principles of organization when unpacking the purchases back home. Organize one's living space for functionality and aesthetics.
- Manage money by structuring a personal budget.

Counseling

- Organize thoughts in decision-making. For example, examine the pros and cons of all the alternatives before making a final choice.
- Examine organizations in terms of their hierarchies, power structures, and rules and regulations, and explore how they impact the individual.

Multicultural

- Experience a day with a colleague or friend from a different country or culture, and observe how that individual's day is organized in terms of events of the day, structure of religious or social rituals, preparation of meals, family hierarchy, or home situations. Record your observations and feelings, and apply your organizational skills to put together a presentation of your experience.

APPLICATION OF ORGANIZATION—ENERGY EFFORTS

The skills involved in organization can be applied in the home setting. For example, consider a family discussing the importance of saving energy and the impact it can have on the planet.

Start with brainstorming ways in which family behaviors and rituals in the home can be organized to minimize energy use—switching off lights which are not needed, taking shorter showers, recycling waste, and so on. Part of this organizational process will involve allocating tasks to various family members. For example, get dad to change shower heads, mom to purchase energy-saving light bulbs, granny to help kids to make a compost heap with left over vegetables and food waste, and so on. This plan can include ways to measure energy-saving efforts and to evaluate the reorganization of lifestyle and behaviors to achieve the goal.

FEUERSTEIN'S THEORY IN MEDIATING ORGANIZATION

Feuerstein's (1980) theory focuses on three areas that impact the development of the thinking skills. These include the *mediated learning experience* (MLE)—the type of interaction initiated by a mediator; the *cognitive functions*—the thinking skills of the learner; and the *cognitive map*—an analysis of the learning task. These three areas provide techniques for analyzing the interaction between the mediator, the learner, and the learning task. They provide a useful framework to use when mediating the thinking skill of *organization*. This can be illustrated using the example of organizing and planning a journey.

Mediated Learning Experience

Feuerstein's (1980) 12 criteria of MLE (see Appendix A) provide the mediator with techniques that help mediate the skill of organizational planning for a journey. Organization is needed to ensure safe and enjoyable travel. For example, mediating *goal planning* will help the learner work systematically through setting and planning an itinerary. Mediating a sense of *challenge* will instill in the learner a feeling of determination and enthusiasm to cope with the novelty and complexity of experiencing new places, different currencies, food, and people.

Cognitive Functions

The list of cognitive functions (see Appendix B) at the input, elaboration, and output phases provide a framework for targeting specific skills needed to ensure effective organization in planning a journey. For example, planning travel arrangements includes ensuring that all the relevant information, such as departure times and accommodation details, are carefully collated (*clear and systematic data-gathering at the input phase*). Similarly, planning needs to be done in a structured and meaningful way (*adequate elaboration of concepts, summative behavior at the elaboration phase*). Finally, a planned and focused response is needed (*appropriate expressive behavior at the output phase*).

Cognitive Map

The cognitive map can be used to analyze and manipulate the learning task to ensure that it is pitched at a meaningful and useful level for the learner (see Appendix C). In this example, planning for travel is an everyday life experience (*content*) using a range of tasks and approaches (*verbal, written, and graphic modalities*) that requires thinking hypothetically about unfamiliar situations, which might prove difficult and challenging (*high levels of abstraction, novelty, and complexity*).

Thus, the techniques of MLE, the cognitive functions, and cognitive map can be used to mediate the skill of *organizing* or planning a journey.

WINDOW TO INTERNATIONAL RESEARCH ON COGNITIVE EDUCATION

Organization of dots is the first instrument used in Feuerstein's (1980) Instrumental Enrichment (IE) program. Overall there are 14 instruments that make up the IE program, which has been implemented in a range of contexts internationally. This extract describes research done using IE with children who have Down syndrome in Israel:

> Feuerstein, Feuerstein, Falik, and Rand (2006) reported that, at the International Centre for the Enhancement of Learning Potential in Jerusalem, an intensive program of Instrumental Enrichment, socialization, training and the creation of modifying environments has helped young adults with Down syndrome develop into individuals who can read and write, serve as volunteers in the army, learn vocational skills and ultimately be gainfully employed as caretakers for the elderly. In one follow-up study of Down syndrome and other developmentally disabled young adults, four to six years following their training in the above-mentioned program and subsequent employment, it was found that 39 of the 40 participants were still gainfully employed, and implementing their training. The authors point out that this constitutes a higher incidence than would be predicted for individuals in similar occupational tracks.

"The reason why most people face the future with apprehension instead of anticipation is because they don't have it well designed."

—Jim Rohn (1994)

2

Comparisons

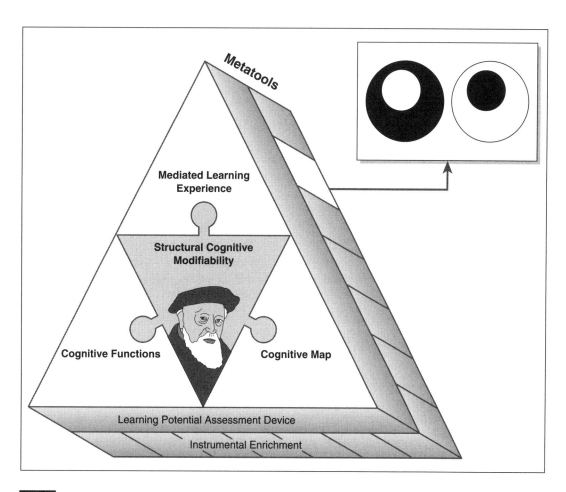

The thinking skill that is discussed in this chapter is *comparison*. Comparisons involve finding similarities and differences between items according to relevant and appropriate criteria. When we compare, we identify what is the same and what is different between things using specific characteristics. For example, an apple and banana both share the characteristic of being a fruit, but they differ in their shape, color, taste, texture, nutrients, and in other ways.

This thinking skill is taught in the *comparisons instrument* of Feuerstein's (1980) Instrumental Enrichment (IE) program. Feuerstein's symbol for the comparisons instrument is two circular figures that have both similar and different attributes. By mentally superimposing one figure over the other, we are able to identify which attributes are similar and which are different. For example, both figures are circles and therefore are similar in shape, but their colors are located in different positions—the one on the left is white on black, and the one on the right is black on white.

COMPARISONS—WHAT, WHY, WHEN, AND WHERE?

How is A related to B? Which is the better? How are they similar and different?

Which should I choose? What decision should I make?

The ability to answer the kinds of questions posed above depends on being able to compare. Comparison is the building block of all relational thinking—understanding how things relate to each other. This involves determining how objects, events, and stimuli are similar and/or different from each other according to different criteria. An effective comparison depends on the relevance and appropriateness of the criteria used for comparison. For example, when selecting players for a sports team, it would be important to compare players based on their ball skills and fitness levels rather than the color of their eyes. Thus the players' skills and abilities are more important criteria to consider than their eye color when selecting a team. Many difficulties with decision making and inappropriate or ill-informed choices can be the result of an inability to use relevant criteria when making a comparison between different options to select. For example, voting for a candidate based on a comparison of the candidates' looks might not be as useful as basing the comparison on their views, values, and intentions.

What Is the Thinking Skill of Comparisons?

Comparison involves identifying and describing what is the same and what is different between objects, events, or ideas according to critical or relevant criteria. For example, when putting together pieces of a puzzle, a black square and a black triangle are compared. The critical criterion for describing the *difference* between these two pieces is shape, whereas the critical criterion for describing *similarity* is color. Choosing the right puzzle piece will depend on using both color and shape as criteria for comparison between pieces.

Why Is the Thinking Skill of Comparisons Important?

There are many reasons to compare. Comparisons provide rich descriptions of events, objects, or feelings in life and enable links and meaningful connections to be made. For example, *happy, elated,* and *ecstatic* all denote different intensities on the same continuum of happiness. Comparisons facilitate decision making by weighing the pros and cons of an argument or by prioritizing criteria used when making a choice between items. For example, when choosing between vacation destinations, criteria such as budget and affordability are higher priorities for consideration than the marketing hype of brochures.

When and Where Is the Thinking Skill of Comparisons Used?

There are numerous contexts where comparison occurs. For example, self-expression and identity development involves defining in what ways we are the same as and different from others. Everyday life decisions involve the act of comparison—for example, choosing what to cook for dinner involves comparing various recipe options based on the criteria of the availability of ingredients, preparation requirements, time factors, and the number of people to feed. Major life decisions—for example, choosing what career to follow, whether to get married, where to live—all involve complex comparisons where the criteria for comparison need to be carefully defined. Celebrating the diversity of cultures in a society and learning to tolerate differences in social practices is based on recognizing and appreciating differences and similarities.

Cognitive Conundrum—Comparisons

There is an old saying that suggests that "comparisons are odious." In some instances, do they force us to become too judgmental and overly critical? Can having too much choice negatively impact our ability to compare rationally? Does it lead to confusion rather than insight when too many criteria have to be considered? What do you think?

BRIDGING COMPARISONS TO FORMAL LEARNING CONTEXTS

Numerous formal learning experiences can be used to mediate comparison.

Humanities

- Critically evaluate the particular bias of opposing political perspectives in history (e.g., different writers' views of an event).
- In literature, find examples of and discuss figures of speech that are based on comparison (e.g., similes, metaphors in poetry).

Social Sciences

- Compare time periods in history (e.g., the Stone Age and Iron Age according to relevant criteria such as lifestyles and work tools).
- Draw comparison charts of different sociogeographical demographics, for example, economies, poverty, imports, and labor markets, and discuss and compare the structures of different types of communities (e.g. urban, suburban, and rural).

Sciences

- Evaluate experiments and support for hypotheses by comparing the conditions and results of experimental and control groups.
- Use the symbols of "greater than" and "less than" to introduce comparisons in mathematical quantities, and compare geometrical shapes according to relevant criteria (number of sides, special angles, properties, etc.).

Arts

- Compare poets and poetry according to themes, style, period, imagery, and other criteria, and encourage art appreciation by comparing techniques, periods, and styles of different artists throughout time.

Technology

- Compare and contrast the different modalities used by young people to communicate with each other—for example, text messaging, MSN, chat rooms, Facebook, MySpace, and YouTube.
- Study and compare the technologies used throughout the ages (e.g., Stone Age, Iron Age, Roman Empire, Middle Ages, and the 20th century).

BRIDGING COMPARISONS TO INFORMAL LEARNING CONTEXTS

General

- Compare and evaluate different teaching techniques (e.g., cooperative learning versus individual learning).
- Compare and evaluate different approaches to taking notes in class (e.g., mind mapping versus taking notes in linear style).

Health and Personal Development

- Compare the outcomes of a healthy lifestyle with those detrimental behaviors that can impact society negatively (e.g., drugs, alcohol misuse, obesity).
- Critically compare the various physical and mental strategies used to obtain Olympic standards—for example, swimming styles, exercise routines, therapies, and sports psychology.

Home

- Enrich outdoor activities by extending an understanding of nature through comparing. For example, compare the needs of different plants—whether or not they need plenty of sun or water, or which plant varieties attract more insects and birds—so that you know where best to plant them.
- Build up a scrapbook with pictures from magazines and newspapers to illustrate a table of the differences and similarities between all the plants and animals in a garden or zoo.

Counseling and Community

- Apply comparisons to aid problem solving. Comparison of positive and negative factors, using various criteria, facilitates thinking through community problems, such as whether a new park or supermarket should be built in the neighborhood; thus, in proposing a park, a criterion such as space may be listed, and the pros and cons of using available space may be discussed.

Multicultural

- Explore the diversity and richness of the different cultures in your community, and compare them according to set criteria (e.g., food, dress, customs, religion, and festivals).

APPLICATION OF COMPARISON—CYBER COUNSELING

The skills involved in comparison can be applied in the counseling setting.

For example, consider how current Internet technology enables individuals to cope with loss, grief, depression, suicidal ideation, and a myriad of other issues through online support groups and counseling websites from the comfort of their own home.

With the exponential growth of online help facilities, it is important that we, as professionals, are able to critically evaluate them. Compare sites such as ShareGrief, the Big White Wall, beyondblue, and so on, in terms of the following criteria: anonymity; confidentiality; user demographic; interaction with professionals; presentation; ease of use; types of feedback; quality and nature of help materials, and so on. The outcomes of these comparisons will help counselors make more informed recommendations to clients.

FEUERSTEIN'S THEORY IN MEDIATING COMPARISON

Feuerstein's (1980) theory focuses on three areas that impact the development of thinking skills. These include the *mediated learning experience* (MLE)—the type of interaction initiated by a mediator; the *cognitive functions*—the thinking skills of the learner; and the *cognitive map*—an analysis of the learning task. These three areas provide techniques for analyzing the interaction between the mediator, the learner, and the learning task. They provide a useful framework when mediating the thinking skill of *comparison.* This can be illustrated using the example of comparing various career options in career counseling.

Mediated Learning Experience

Feuerstein's (1980) 12 criteria of MLE (see Appendix A) provide the mediator with techniques that help mediate the skill of comparison when deciding between different career options. Mediating *self-regulation* and *control of behavior* will help the learner control impulsivity and self-monitor in order to take the time to explore the range of career options according to relevant criteria and guard against foreclosure in career choice. Mediating a sense of *challenge* will instill determination and enthusiasm in the learner to explore new and different career opportunities.

Cognitive Functions

The list of cognitive functions (see Appendix B) at the input, elaboration, and output phases give a framework for targeting specific skills needed to ensure effective comparisons when selecting and comparing different careers. Comparing different career options involves focusing on a variety of criteria such as degree requirements, skills needed, type of work, environment, pay scale, and so on (*considering more than one source of information at the input phase*) in order to make sound judgments (*addressing the need for logical evidence at the elaboration phase*) and systematically testing job opportunities (*working through output responses at the output phase*).

Cognitive Map

The cognitive map can be used to analyze and manipulate the learning task to ensure that it is pitched at a meaningful and useful level for the learner (see Appendix C). In this example, choosing between career options is an everyday life experience (*content*) using a range of tasks and approaches (*verbal, written, and graphic modalities*) that requires looking at similarities and differences between different career options (*medium levels of abstraction, novelty, and complexity*).

Thus, the techniques of MLE, the cognitive functions, and the cognitive map can be used to mediate the skill of *comparison* in career counseling.

WINDOW TO INTERNATIONAL RESEARCH ON COGNITIVE EDUCATION

Comparison is the second instrument used in Feuerstein's Instrumental Enrichment (IE) Program. Overall, there are 14 instruments that make up the IE program, which has been implemented in a range of contexts internationally. This extract describes research done using IE in the United States of America:

> Ben-Hur (2000) noted that IE has been disseminated in the United States since 1978. He reported that in the United States thousands of teachers have been trained to use IE, and each year about 10,000 students benefit from it. Evaluations have yielded very positive results in a variety of academic and nonacademic areas, including inter alia students' ability to learn and their academic performance.

The positive impact on the student's academic performance has been consistently reported where schools integrate IE into the curriculum and use it to guide a systemic reform. Ben-Hur considered the best example of this to be the IE project in Taunton, Massachusetts (Williams & Kopp, 1994), where all third to fifth graders received the program. The ethos of IE also pervaded the schools. During that period, significant gains were made in the following areas: a decrease in student dropout rate; improvement in school attendance; decrease in out-of-district placement costs; and cumulative increases in reading comprehension scores for the IE group relative to those of a control group.

"There is no teaching to compare with example."

—Robert Powell

3

Categorization

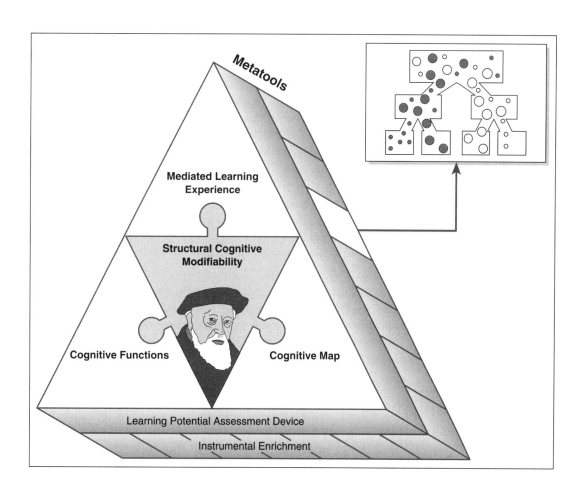

The thinking skill that is discussed in this chapter is *categorization*. Categorization involves grouping elements according to appropriate principles. When we categorize, we place items into particular classes or groups. For example, members of a choir are grouped into section depending on the pitch of their voice.

The thinking skill of categorization is taught in the *categorization instrument* of Feuerstein's (1980) Instrumental Enrichment (IE) program. Feuerstein's symbol for the categorization instrument shows how a mixed group of circles can be divided into subgroups according to the principles of color and size. Four categories can then be created from the large, unsorted group. These subgroups of circles are small/black, large/black, large/white, and small/white. The arrows created by space at the bottom point upward to indicate that the process can be reversed to reconstruct the original group

CATEGORIZATION—WHAT, WHY, WHEN, AND WHERE?

What are the different genres of poetry, music, and literature? How are animals classified into vertebrates and invertebrates in zoology? Show the grouping of family members across generations.

The ability to answer these kinds of questions depends on the thinking skill of categorization. Categorization involves grouping elements according to relevant principles (e.g., sorting laundry into piles of whites, colored items, and hand-washables). Such ordering makes our lives more efficient and structured. This skill builds on the previous two thinking skills of organization and comparison. Organization involves overcoming an episodic grasp of reality and seeing the relationships between stimuli. Comparison involves identifying the similarities and differences between those related stimuli. Categorization extends these skills by grouping similar stimuli into groups and subgroups. Categories can be represented by flow charts, Venn diagrams, tables, or grids. Careful consideration is needed to define categories accurately in order to avoid overinclusion or underinclusion of members or items in a category. For example, oranges, lemons, and apples belong in the category identified as fruit, but are overincluded in the category of citrus fruit (as apples are not citrus) and underincluded in the category of food (as many other nonfruit items also belong in this category). Categorization thus involves defining the group accurately and selecting members of the group based on this definition.

What Is the Thinking Skill of Categorization?

Categorization involves establishing sets or groups, based on the commonalities among elements and subsets or subgroups, based on the differences between members. For example, students might be grouped into a set based on the commonality of their ages, and into subsets based on their different reading abilities. Categories are not always fixed and can change depending on the criteria or principals. Categories are not the only way of organizing information—in some instances a continuum rather than discrete groups may be more relevant. For example, categorizing according to gender might result in a fixed stable group, but categorizing according to interests or experience or affect will result in changes of group members over time, as their membership is more flexible, contextualized, or subjective. Care also needs to be taken not to stereotype—which involves ascribing to all members of the group certain qualities that might only relate to some—when categorizing.

Why Is the Thinking Skill of Categorization Important?

There are many reasons to categorize. Categorization helps to organize information—for example, books in a library are organized into categories such as fiction and non-fiction. Constructing flow charts and tables of course content as an aid to studying facilitates remembering information. Categorizing enables us to be economical and efficient—for example, the sections of the newspaper provides quick and easy access to information. Understanding group membership is a way to gain insight into the way society functions—for example, when race or gender is inappropriately used as the basis of discriminating against certain groups or categories of people. Grouping accurately, by not overincluding or underincluding, is a way to clarify and gain deeper understanding of information—for example, behaviorism can be grouped under the category of learning theory, which is a subcategory of educational psychology.

When and Where Is the Thinking Skill of Categorization Used?

There are numerous contexts where there are opportunities to develop the skill of categorization. In the home setting, for example, packing away toys into containers according to the type, color, or size will provide toddlers with practice in discriminating between items. In the school context, sorting into groups and subgroups develops understanding of the complexities of categorization—for example, grammatical analysis of sentences into the group on nouns and subgroups of proper and common nouns. Making judgments and decisions in everyday life is enhanced through using categorization skills—for example, making choices of right and wrong according to the principles of what is legal and/or moral, and so on.

Cognitive Conundrum—Categorization

It has been argued that by grouping individuals or objects into categories, we detract from their individuality and truly unique essence. There is a thought that categorization leads to a form of stereotyping—"grouping all under one umbrella." What do you think?

BRIDGING CATEGORIZATION TO FORMAL LEARNING CONTEXTS

Numerous formal learning experiences can be used to mediate categorization.

Humanities

- Group spelling words that have similar phonemes together in order to facilitate accurate recall (e.g., *boat, coat, float*).
- Group similar parts of speech from a passage of text (e.g., grouping all the nouns and verbs, and then making subgroups: e.g., common nouns and proper nouns; state-of-being and action verbs).

Social Sciences

- Tabulate content information by grouping into sections (e.g., World War I can be categorized according to allies, causes, battles, and famous people).
- Teach history through themes (e.g., laws, period costumes, and transportation).
- Design categorization tables to show how different political orientations can be grouped (e.g., right wing and left wing, and within each of these, progressive or conservative).

Sciences

- Show how the periodic table groups elements such as metals and nonmetals according to their chemical properties, and group substances into the various states of matter (e.g., solids, liquids, gases, and plasma).
- Use Venn diagrams in geometry to show how members are classified into sets and subsets (e.g., all four-sided shapes—rhombus, trapezium, square, rectangle).

Arts

- Categorize all the possible avenues or mediums of an art form (e.g., graphics—etchings, lithographs; sculpture—clay, iron; painting—oil, water), and then review the classification of artists utilizing these media categories.
- Classify musical instruments into types (e.g., percussion, string, and wind), and review their groupings and arrangement in an orchestra.

Technology

- Review how we conduct Internet research by using broad categories that become more finely focused into sets and subsets until we isolate a specific URL or website.

BRIDGING CATEGORIZATION TO INFORMAL LEARNING CONTEXTS

General

- Structure overviews of the course work for the year in different subjects by grouping them into main sections and subsections.
- Demonstrate how different university courses or vocations can be categorized by the use of various criteria—skills, qualifications, talents, and so on.
- Categorization can be used creatively by changing the criteria for inclusion and exclusion within sets and looking for less obvious criteria. For example, consider the type of questions in the Twenty Questions game.

Health and Personal Development

- Analyze the formation of social groups in your school or business. Consider the criteria that mark a specific social group—goths, emos, nerds, and so on, and how you fit in personally.
- Categorize sports according to specific aspects such as skills needed, apparatus used, types of training, muscles structures that have to be built, and other criteria.

Home

- Play games, which require children to identify "the odd one out" of a category.
- Sort silverware into correct trays (i.e., knives, forks, spoons) or clothes into correct drawers (e.g., socks, underwear, T–shirts).

Counseling

- Narrow down and identify groups of career options (e.g., looking at groups of careers in terms of values, interests, and abilities).
- Recognize that "smaller bits are easier to handle" and reduce stress (e.g., enhancing study skills by dividing data into areas that make them easier to remember and recall).

Multicultural

- Set up an activity in which students research customs and values within different cultures under specific categories, such as food, music, literature, or medicine. For example, in the Orthodox Jewish religious culture, traditions are maintained through food (kosher), literature (the Torah), and music (liturgy).

APPLICATION OF
CATEGORIZATION—TOYS AND TOTS

The skills involved in categorization can be applied in the early childhood education setting. For example, consider toddlers and their interaction with various toys.

While toddlers are playing with toys such as blocks, Legos, and so on, encourage them to assemble structures of varying designs according to different criteria. For example, building a tower using only the rectangular blocks (criterion of shape) or only the blue blocks (criterion of color). Extend their concept of categorization by combining two criteria in their sorting—for example, collecting all the red squares (criteria of color and shape).

FEUERSTEIN'S THEORY IN MEDIATING CATEGORIZATION

Feuerstein's (1980) theory focuses on three areas that impact on the development of the thinking skills. These include the *mediated learning experience* (MLE)—the type of interaction initiated by a mediator; the *cognitive functions*—the thinking skills of the learner; and the *cognitive map*—an analysis of the learning task. These three areas provide techniques for analyzing the interaction between the mediator, the learner, and the learning task. They provide a useful framework to use when mediating the thinking skill of *categorization.* This can be illustrated using the example of stock-taking and stacking shelves in a warehouse or storeroom.

Mediated Learning Experience

Feuerstein's (1980) 12 criteria of MLE (see Appendix A) provide the mediator with techniques that help mediate the skill of categorization when sorting items to stack on shelves in a storeroom. Mediating *meaning and transcendence* will encourage the learner to recognize the underlying purpose and principles of grouping certain similar items together and enable this skill to be used in other contexts. For example, categorizing items results in knowing what is available, and where and how to access the item. This skill of categorization can be applied to other situations, for example, in grouping study content, sorting home contents, or cleaning and sorting the shed.

Cognitive Functions

The list of cognitive functions (see Appendix B) at the input, elaboration, and output phases give a framework for targeting specific skills needed to categorize items efficiently. For example, initial sorting of items involves analyzing and discriminating between the different characteristics of items (*considering more than one source of information at the input phase*). Each item is evaluated in terms of whether it fits into a particular category or group (*engaging in spontaneous comparative behavior at the elaboration phase*) so as to minimize the chances of an incorrect grouping (*trial-and-error response at the output phase*).

Cognitive Map

The cognitive map can be used to analyze and manipulate the learning task to ensure that it is pitched at a meaningful and useful level for the learner (see Appendix C). In this example, sorting items into groups is an everyday life experience (*content*) that involves physical sorting of concrete items (*tactile and kinesthetic modalities*) which is a concrete, relatively familiar, and easy task (*low levels of abstraction, novelty, and complexity*).

Thus the techniques of MLE, the cognitive functions, and cognitive map can be used to mediate the skill of categorizing items for stocktaking and stacking.

WINDOW TO INTERNATIONAL RESEARCH ON COGNITIVE EDUCATION

Categorization is the third instrument used in Feuerstein's (1980) Instrumental Enrichment (IE) program. Overall, there are 14 instruments that make up the IE program, which has been implemented in a range of contexts internationally. This extract describes research done using IE with underserved minority students in the United States of America:

Recently, a joint Instrumental Enrichment project was initiated between Feuerstein's International Centre for the Enhancement of Learning Potential in Israel and the National Urban Alliance (NUA) in the United States. Cooper (2007) reported that NUA's mission is to close the achievement gap for America's urban students by working with local school district administrators and teachers to ensure that all students receive high-quality instruction in all academic subjects. IE is seen as one of the means to achieving this goal. Initially, it involves the implementation of the IE program in schools in 20 U.S. cities. The intention is to improve student achievement, especially of Black children, and involves a "special concern for underserved and underperforming Black males in the United States," (Cooper, 2007). Students of African American and Hispanic background will take part at various elementary schools in the selected districts of these cities. Cooper considers that IE will assist in counteracting the misdiagnosis of a disproportionate number of minority children as needing special education. He indicated that the large body of research data attesting to IE's positive outcomes provided the impetus for this project.

"Class, race, sexuality, gender, and all other categories by which we categorize and dismiss each other need to be excavated from the inside."
—Dorothy Allison

4

Relational
Orientation
in Space

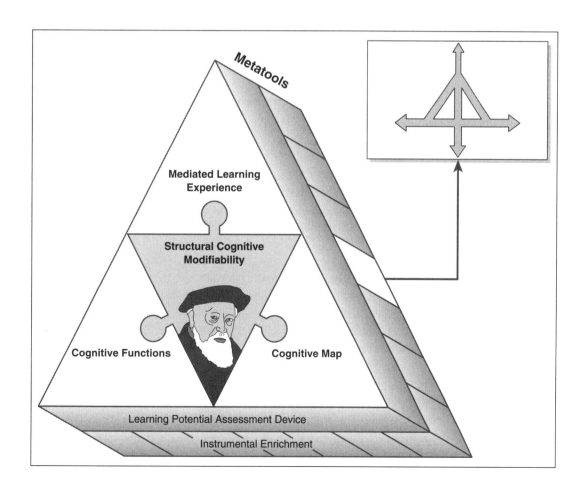

The thinking skill that is discussed in this chapter is *relational orientation in space.* Orientation in Space involves understanding how objects relate to one another in space. *Orientation* can be described as having an understanding of one's relative position or being familiar with one's surroundings (the opposite of being disoriented). *Space* can be described as an expanse or area in which objects exist or move. Space includes the individual's immediate surroundings, the classroom, school, town, world, and universe, extending ever outwards. Understanding one's relative position in space depends on an internal reference system—the direction that one is facing. The direction that one is facing will determine where *up, down, left, right, back,* and *front* are—relative to oneself. Thus one's orientation in space is determined in relation to the direction one is facing or one's internal reference system.

This thinking skill is taught in the *orientation in space I instrument* of Feuerstein's (1980) Instrumental Enrichment (IE) program. Feuerstein's symbol for the orientation in space instrument is depicted by crossroads from which four arrows point in four different directions. It introduces the terms *left, right, back,* and *front.* The instrument provides practice in identifying direction and orientation based on where items are in relation to other items in space.

RELATIONAL ORIENTATION IN SPACE—WHAT, WHY, WHEN, AND WHERE?

> *Which is the quickest route to town? Where is the fiction section of the library? If I turned 45 degrees to the right, what would be in front of me and behind me?*

Being able to answer these kinds of questions depends on the ability to orient oneself in space through understanding relational positions and directions. This involves having an internalized system of reference for describing objects and events in space and appreciating that the description of the position of objects is determined in relation to each other.

Having a good orientation in space at the concrete or physical level can be bridged to an abstract or psychological level. At the physical level, orientation involves understanding that left, right, back, front, up and down are relative—depending on the way you are facing. If you change position, these directions change relative to your new position. At the psychological level, orientation involves understanding that one's perspective on an issue is also subjective and relative. Being able to see things from a different orientation or putting oneself in the shoes of another involves being able to shift direction or perspective at a psychological level and appreciation that there are many views or perspectives on a single issue. What is conservative for one person is liberal for another. What is right or moral for one culture might be wrong or immoral for another. *Empathic understanding* is when one is able to move beyond one's personal perspective and appreciate another's point of view. Thus, understanding relativity in one's physical orientation can translate into understanding different psychological orientations.

What Is the Thinking Skill of Relational Orientation in Space?

Relational orientation in space enables us to describe relationships among objects and among events in space. It involves developing an internalized reference system to describe what is to the left, right, back, and front in order to locate oneself in space. Orientation relates to being able to organize the physical environment and being aware that directions are relative and not fixed or static. For example, if two people are facing each other, then objects to the right of one person are automatically to the left of the other person. What is in front for one is at the back for the other. Orientation is relative to the direction one is facing and depends on one's internal reference system.

Why Is the Thinking Skill of Relational Orientation in Space Important?

There are many reasons why teaching relational orientation in space is important. Spatial orientation promotes relational thinking—an understanding that relationships between things are relative and not fixed. For example, if I turn 180 degrees left, then what was on my left is now on my right. Thus, directions need to be interpreted carefully, as they are dependent on the position one is facing. Spatial orientation develops metacognitive awareness of one's perspective on issues and a realization of the relativity of this view. Teaching relational thinking helps to develop empathic thinking or empathy, which involves seeing things from another's point of view or putting yourself in someone else's shoes to see things from their perspective.

When and Where is Relational Orientation in Space Used?

There are numerous contexts where relational orientation in space occurs. For example, physical orientation involves understanding directions (left, right, back, and front) and being able to move about in an area without getting lost or causing accidents. Psychological orientation relates to listening to someone else's point of view or appreciating how perspectives can differ. This involves seeing things from a different orientation.

Cognitive Conundrum—Relational Orientation in Space

By setting up fixed paths (set orientations) to follow in life because of constraints on time, emotion, cost, and so on, are we hampering our ability to explore "the road less traveled"? What do you think?

BRIDGING RELATIONAL ORIENTATION IN SPACE TO FORMAL LEARNING CONTEXTS

Numerous formal learning experiences can be used to mediate relational orientation in space.

Humanities

- Identify prepositions that indicate a specific orientation (e.g., *in, on, over, under*).
- Appreciate literature and poetry through exploring the different characters' perspectives.
- Encourage the use of precise vocabulary when giving directions or explaining one's point of view.
- Highlight the biases of different historians, writers, or journalists in describing events.

Social Sciences

- Describe and discuss political terms (e.g., *left wing* and *right wing, liberal* and *conservative*).
- Discuss different perspectives of an event that has greatly impacted society (e.g., destruction of the Twin Towers in New York, fall of the Berlin Wall, genocide in Uganda).
- Map out routes traveled to and from school or work everyday. Draw these maps from different orientations in space (e.g., aerial and lateral views), and then explore the sociopsychological aspects of adopting specific routes (e.g., avoiding the frustration of traffic jams on congested streets).

Sciences

- Practice drawing diagrams of animals, plants, and laboratory apparatuses from different orientations (e.g., a cross-section or transverse section).

Arts

- Visualize and sketch the same object from four different perspectives.
- Explore the concept of symmetry in art forms and objects. Try to map left and right.

Technology

- Structure logarithms that direct a mechanical robot arm to perform a specific operation that demands changes in orientation.

BRIDGING RELATIONAL ORIENTATION IN SPACE TO INFORMAL LEARNING CONTEXTS

General

- Discuss the feeling of disorientation when in unfamiliar surroundings.
- Use games to find directions from different starting points.
- Practice changing one's orientation by describing different points of view.

Health and Personal Development

- Encourage individuals to explore specific social and psychological problems from various perspectives (e.g., substance misuse, bullying, self-harm, eating disorders).
- Work with young children on sets of exercises that demand strength and coordination of both sides of the body and develop an understanding of their positioning in space.

Home

- Create a game that involves remembering the route between home and various other locations often visited, such as school, local shops, the homes of grandparents, or the homes of friends.
- Play a game where everyone can shut their eyes and try to imagine a particular route (e.g., who can recall the most landmarks along the way?).
- Put on the left and right shoes correctly (physical orientation), arrange place settings at the dining room or kitchen table, and create an understanding environment with other people in the household (psychological orientation); all develop orientation skills.

Counseling

- Set up a scenario where students who have strong relationships form pairs. Each member of the pair discusses how he or she views the other. Partners then compare their views. Have they been fair to each other?

Multicultural

- Use the skills in spatial orientation to explore different cultures. Describe aspects such as
  - Family structures (single-parent households, "traditional" families, etc.)
  - Women's roles
  - Place of and attitude toward the elderly in society
  - Political or socioeconomic status of the group within society

APPLICATION OF RELATIONAL ORIENTATION IN SPACE—FAMILY FEUDS

The skills involved in relational orientation in space can be applied to the family counseling setting. For example, consider the impact of conflicting perspectives in family feuds.

An ability to apply relational, hypothetical, and empathic thinking can help resolve conflicts between family members. In family counseling, for instance, allow each individual to assume a role and discuss it in terms of the perceptions of other members of the family. Individuals can explore how realistic and fair their expectations of each other are. An individual can assume the role usually taken by another family member in order to appreciate the perspectives of that family member. As a result, they can try to reorient their thinking and expectations regarding the problem.

FEUERSTEIN'S THEORY IN MEDIATING RELATIONAL ORIENTATION IN SPACE

Feuerstein's (1980) theory focuses on three areas that impact the development of the thinking skills. These include the *mediated learning experience* (MLE)—the type of interaction initiated by a mediator; the *cognitive functions*—the thinking skills of the learner; and the *cognitive map*—an analysis of the learning task. These three areas provide techniques for analyzing the interaction between the mediator, the learner, and the learning task. They provide a useful framework to use when mediating the thinking skill of *relational orientation in space.* This can be illustrated using the example of reading a roadmap.

Mediated Learning Experience

Feuerstein's (1980) 12 criteria of MLE (see Appendix A) provide the mediator with techniques that help mediate the skill of finding an address by reading a road map. This is dependent upon an understanding of the relativity of positions and an appreciation that following directions effectively is dependent on the way one is facing. Mediating *intentionality* and *reciprocity* will focus the learner on the given task. Mediating *individuation* will encourage the learner to understand the unique orientation that each individual has and that this is relative and changeable depending upon one's position, stance, or direction.

Cognitive Functions

The list of cognitive functions (see Appendix B) at the input, elaboration, and output phases give a framework for targeting specific skills needed to be effective in navigating by using a road map. At the outset, a learner needs to understand the relative concepts of left and right (*understanding spatial concepts at the input phase*). Once they are comfortable with the notion that left and right change relative to the position one is facing, they need to locate their own position on the map and mentally transfer directions (*projecting virtual relations at the elaboration phase*). This will result in effective reading of the map and overcome any confusion or getting lost (*overcoming trail and error responses at the output phase*).

Cognitive Map

The cognitive map can be used to analyze and manipulate the learning task to ensure that it is pitched at a meaningful and useful level for the learner (see Appendix C). In this example, finding directions is an everyday life experience (*content*) presented as a roadmap (*diagrammatic modality*) that requires understanding the relativity of right, left, back, and front (*medium levels of abstraction, novelty, and complexity*).

Thus the techniques of MLE, the cognitive functions, and cognitive map can be used to mediate the skill of *relational orientation in space* in map reading.

WINDOW TO INTERNATIONAL RESEARCH ON COGNITIVE EDUCATION

Orientation in Space I is the fourth instrument used in Feuerstein's (1980) Instrumental Enrichment (IE) program. Overall, there are 14 instruments that make up the IE program, which has been implemented in a range of contexts internationally. This extract describes research done using IE in elementary and junior high schools in Canada:

Mulcahy (1994) conducted a study in a school district of Alberta, Canada. The two-year IE project involved a population of 900 students that started IE in the fourth and the seventh grades. The sample was divided into three treatment groups, namely (1) IE; (2) The Strategies Program for Effective Learning/ Thinking (developed by one of the researchers); and (3) the traditional curriculum and instruction (control) group.

Findings were that IE students' achievement on tests of mathematical concepts and applications was significantly better than that of the control group. It was also found that the cognitive strategies utilized by students in both experimental (cognitive education) groups increased significantly after instruction, as did their degree of metacognitive reading awareness. The comprehension skills of students after two years of instruction in the two cognitive education programs were observed to be generally better than their control counterparts. The findings led the author to stress the need for a comprehensive and integrated approach to the teaching of cognitive strategies across all levels of education—from kindergarten to postsecondary.

"What was most significant about the lunar voyage was not that men set foot on the moon, but that they set eye on Earth"

—Norman Cousins

"There is probably no oral society that fails to mark the spatial distinction of left and right, peculiar as this distinction may be."

—David Antin

5

Cardinal
Orientation
in Space

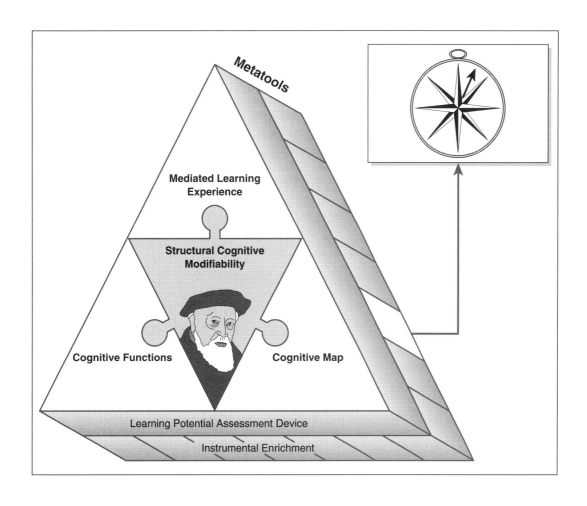

The thinking skill that is outlined in this chapter is *cardinal orientation in space.* This is an extension of the skill discussed in the previous chapter, relational orientation in space. While relational orientation in space showed how directions (left, right, back, and front) were relative and dependent on an internal reference system, cardinal orientation in space introduces the learner to the cardinal compass points—north, south, east, and west—and shows how these are fixed, absolute, and external to the individual.

The thinking skill of cardinal orientation in space is taught in the *orientation in space II instrument* of Feuerstein's (1980) Instrumental Enrichment (IE) program. Feuerstein's symbol for the orientation in space II instrument is the compass rose, showing the points of N, NE, E, SE, S, SW, W, and NW. This symbol depicts the universal and absolute characteristic of using compass points when describing a position in space.

CARDINAL ORIENTATION IN SPACE—WHAT, WHY, WHEN, AND WHERE?

> *Where are we on this map? Where does the sun rise and set?*
>
> *How can I give a precise and constant description of positions?*

The ability to answer these kinds of questions depends on having a good understanding of cardinal points (north, south, east, and west). This is what is described in cardinal orientation in space. In relational orientation in space, the terms *left, right, back,* and *front* were introduced to show how objects relate to one another in space. Using that reference system, orientations are relative to individual positions (e.g., if I turn around, then what is in front of me becomes what is behind me). However, in cardinal orientation in space, the points of the compass—north, south, east, and west—are used. This reference system is absolute (e.g., north does not change if I turn around or change my position). The compass points are an objective, stable, and universally accepted manner of describing locations.

What Is the Thinking Skill of Cardinal Orientation in Space?

Cardinal orientation in space teaches the skill of describing a position in space accurately by using the compass points of north, south, east, and west. This instrument involves recognizing that the compass-point reference system is external and absolute. In this system orientation, direction or position is not dependent on the relative position of the referent—the individual or object. The compass-point reference system is accurate, precise, and universal. It is a convention used throughout the world, and it is standardized.

Why Is the Thinking Skill of
Cardinal Orientation in Space Important?

There are numerous reasons why it is important to teach the thinking skills of cardinal orientation in space. The compass points provide a reference system that affords an accurate description of the position of objects in space. They constitute a system of reference that is universal and absolute. Using both the absolute, external system of compass points (north, south, east, and west) in conjunction with the relative, internal system (left, right, back, and front) allows for flexibility when describing positions. Cardinal orientation in space can be used to bridge the concept that some rules are absolute or fixed and are interpreted universally in the same way—for example scientific laws or musical notation.

When and Where Is the Thinking Skill
of Cardinal Orientation in Space Used?

There are numerous contexts and situations where we use cardinal orientation in space. Using compass directions enables an accurate and precise description of the location of something, which in some instances is a matter of life and death—for example a ship in distress needing to be rescued or navigating a difficult terrain where the physical features can be misleading in terms of which direction to follow. Directions often need to be communicated in a universal language, for example, drawing maps or plotting trajectories or movements in space.

As suggested in the previous chapter on relational orientation in space, understanding physical space facilitates appreciation of psychological space. Bridging this concept to cardinal orientation in space, it raises the notion that different psychological perspectives and orientations to things can change around a fixed point of view. For example, a liberal point of view is always to the "left" of a conservative point of view; a pessimistic interpretation to an event or situation is always seeing the worst, and an optimistic orientation is always seeing the best in a situation.

Cognitive Conundrum—Cardinal Orientation in Space

There is some conjecture regarding the increased usage of personal navigation instruments in our motor vehicles. The feeling is that they are destroying our own natural and instinctual ability to find direction and orient in space. We seem to have lost what animals have retained so strongly—an innate ability to find our way! What do you think?

BRIDGING CARDINAL ORIENTATION IN SPACE TO FORMAL LEARNING CONTEXTS

Numerous formal learning experiences can be used to mediate cardinal orientation in space.

Humanities

- Create opportunities for students to structure verbal maps to direct one another along different routes, using fixed landmarks as a reference.
- Select and comment on poetry that incorporates the cardinal points of the compass.

Social Sciences

- Find animal habitats and plants that have a particular orientation for survival (e.g., migration of whales to Antarctica; sunflowers moving their heads to capture the sun's rays).
- Explain how to use a compass and the difference between magnetic north and true north.
- Study how the earth is divided by imaginary lines of latitude and longitude and the degrees of change in them. Talk about how this impacts our communication and travel across the globe.
- Contrast how groups of people have been named according to their cardinal and/or geographic domain (e.g., Northerners, South Africans, North American Indians, Eastern Europeans).

Sciences

- Explain the concept of earth's gravity and how it affects our lives. Contrast with gravity in outer space.
- Demonstrate coordinate geometry by plotting x and y points on a graph.
- Draw angles of different degrees, showing how 0° and 360° are north. Discuss their use in navigation.

Arts

- Design a building that takes into consideration the aesthetic and practical implications of the location (e.g., a north-facing house in the southern hemisphere).
- Examine how an orchestra is controlled from a fixed point by the conductor's hand, arm, and body directions and movements.

Technology

- Read up on green architecture and how some new buildings have been designed to maximize on energy saving by being oriented around cardinal points and axes.

BRIDGING CARDINAL ORIENTATION IN SPACE TO INFORMAL LEARNING CONTEXTS

General

- Draw patterns using a Spirograph, which has a fixed central point.
- Copy pictures using a grid and the compass points as a guide.

Health and Personal Development

- Explore the idea of *emotional coordinates* by answering the question, Where do I place myself today in terms of happiness? Show that although the emotional coordinate is fixed, the reasons for happiness are dynamic (e.g., Monday is a school day; on Wednesday a favorite sport is played; Saturday is a day for going to the movies with friends).
- Give a course in orienteering to students as a team-building exercise. Choose an unfamiliar environment where they need to use compass directions to find their way home.

Home

- Show children how to make a drawing of their house from different cardinal aspects (e.g., from the north side and from the south side).
- Follow a pattern or design, such as one for embroidery, by numbering squares on a grid.
- Plan an ideal kitchen, considering the fact that plumbing and electricity may need to remain in fixed positions.
- Set up a sundial to show the direction of north, and watch how the relationship between sun and shadow changes.
- Construct a model following a grid plan.

Counseling

- Discuss the concept of "rules of life" in counseling (i.e., the idea that certain laws that govern our lives are fixed, and we have to orientate our thinking to work within them).

APPLICATION OF CARDINAL ORIENTATION IN SPACE—CULTURAL COMPASS

The skills involved in cardinal orientation in space can be applied in the classroom setting. For example, consider a classroom of children of mixed cultures talking about where they come from—east, west, south, or north parts of the country, or the world.

External, stable, and absolute systems of reference can be used to highlight and appreciate the differences between cultures that exist in different continents of the world. For example, research the indigenous tribes of Africa or North America and discuss how their geographical orientation on Earth relates to their customs and cultural characteristics. Also explore the various cultural orientations within the classroom. Review the differences in, for instance, Eastern and Western customs in terms of their global orientation (e.g., facing Mecca for prayer, bowing to the sunrise, Yogic salutations to the sun, following lunar patterns in northern and southern hemispheres).

FEUERSTEIN'S THEORY IN MEDIATING CARDINAL ORIENTATION IN SPACE

Feuerstein's (1980) theory focuses on three areas that impact the development of the thinking skills. These include the *mediated learning experience* (MLE)—the type of interaction initiated by a mediator; the *cognitive functions*—the thinking skills of the learner; and the *cognitive map*—an analysis of the learning task. These three areas provide techniques for analyzing the interaction between the mediator, the learner, and the learning task. They provide a useful framework to use when mediating the thinking skill of *cardinal orientation in space*. This can be illustrated using the example of identifying different geographical areas using the north, south, east, and west cardinal constants.

Mediated Learning Experience

Feuerstein's 12 criteria of MLE (see Appendix A) provide the mediator with techniques that help mediate the skill of cardinal orientation in space. For example, mediating *goal planning* will encourage working in an ordered and sequential way to plot the compass coordinates of each geographical area. Mediating a sense of *challenge* will instill in the learner a feeling of determination to learn to use a compass confidently and competently.

Cognitive Functions

The list of cognitive functions (see Appendix B) at the input, elaboration, and output phases give a framework for targeting specific skills needed to plot cardinal points in identifying different geographical orientations. For example, accuracy and attention to details is essential so that data is correctly collated (*clear and systematic data gathering at the input phase*). In executing the task, planning needs to be done in a structured and sequential way (*appropriate planning behavior, adequate elaboration of concepts, need for logical evidence, and hypothesis testing at the elaboration phase*). Finally, a planned and focused response is needed (*appropriate expressive behavior at the output phase*), rather than blocking, impulsive, or trial-and-error behavior.

Cognitive Map

The cognitive map can be used to analyze and manipulate the learning task to ensure that it is pitched at a meaningful and useful level for the learner (see Appendix C). In this example, plotting coordinates is an advanced spatial task (*content*) using a compass and grid (*spatial and graphic modality*) that requires understanding the static nature of north, south, east, and west (*high levels of abstraction, novelty and complexity*).

Thus, the techniques of MLE, the cognitive functions, and cognitive map can be used to mediate the skill of cardinal orientation in space in using the north, south, east, and west cardinal constants.

WINDOW TO INTERNATIONAL
RESEARCH ON COGNITIVE EDUCATION

Orientation in Space II is the fifth instrument used in Feuerstein's (1980) Instrumental Enrichment (IE) program. Overall, there are 14 instruments that make up the IE program, which has been implemented in a range of contexts internationally. This extract describes research done using IE for students with behavioral and emotional difficulties in the United Kingdom:

In 2005, a project in IE was instituted by the Scottish Borders Education Council under whose auspices a pilot study was conducted by Dr. R. Soden of Strathclyde University. The pilot project included 32 primary and secondary teachers, including members of school senior management teams. Also included in the study were 67 students from the 5th to the 10th grades, most of whom had a history of poor scholastic achievement due to social, emotional, or behavioral problems. Findings included, inter alia, the following: increases for over three quarters of the sample in aspects of cognitive functioning connected with school attainment targeted; effectiveness in facilitating relationship-building and enhancing focus on teaching objectives; increases in motivation and confidence towards learning relative to control students; raised awareness and enhanced reflective practice among teachers, particularly in relation to cognitive functions and tackling deficiencies; a significant shift in attitudes and behavior towards learners. The evaluation report concluded that the approach offers a coherent whole-school approach to raising ability and attainment, and continuation of the IE program throughout the schools in the district was supported.

"Now my eyes are turned from the South to the North, and I want to lead one more Expedition. This will be the last . . . to the North Pole."

—Ernest Shackleton

"We all live under the same sky, but we don't have the same horizon"

—Konrad Adenauer

6

Analysis and Synthesis

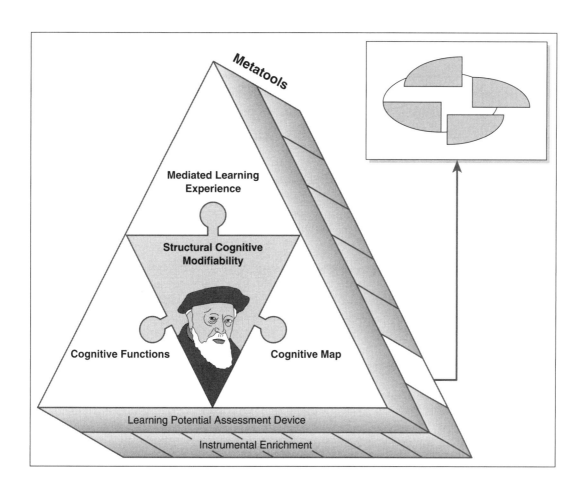

Throe thinking skill that is outlined in this chapter is *analysis and synthesis*. Analysis and synthesis involves the skill of breaking the whole into its parts (analysis) and putting the parts together to make a whole (synthesis). Analysis involves breaking up an organized entity so that the sections stand out and are separate from each other, for example identifying the nouns and verbs in a sentence, cutting out the parts of a dress, or laying out the pieces of a puzzle. Synthesis involves organizing the parts into a meaningful whole or restructuring them into a new and original whole, for example in making a sentence, dressmaking, or assembling a model airplane.

The thinking skills of analysis and synthesis are taught in the *analytic perception instrument* of Feuerstein's (1980) Instrumental Enrichment (IE) program. Feuerstein's symbol for the analytic perception instrument is an ellipse that has been divided into four quarters. It illustrates that an item can be divided into sections according to relevant criteria. While this symbol focuses predominantly on analysis, the inverse is true too—the four quarters can combine again to form an ellipse, synthesizing the parts.

ANALYSIS AND SYNTHESIS—
WHAT, WHY, WHEN, AND WHERE?

How can I fix this broken tool? Which paint colors must I mix to get green? How many study hours are there in a day? Which piece of the puzzle fits where?

The ability to answer these kinds of questions depends on the thinking skill of analysis and synthesize. This involves asking the following questions: What are the parts? What are the steps involved in the process? and How are the parts related to each other and to the whole?

> "Analysis and synthesis, though commonly treated as two different methods, are, if properly understood, only the two necessary parts of the same method. Each is the relative and correlative of the other."
>
> —Sir W. Hamilton

What Is the Thinking Skill of Analysis and Synthesis?

Analysis involves dividing a whole into its parts according to relevant criteria (differentiation). Synthesis involves joining the parts together to make a meaningful whole (integration). In order to adapt and function successfully in the world, we need to develop a good balance between the two processes of differentiation and integration. Understanding the underlying principles, mores, codes, or process that govern the structure of the whole will provide the insight necessary to engage in differentiation and integration. Both analysis and synthesis are involved, alternately, in all aspects of cognition. This can be liked to the Piagetian concepts of *assimilation*—taking on board new "bits" or pieces of information and knowledge—and *accommodation*—integrating the new bits into a new understanding of how the parts interact and link with each other to form a whole.

Why Is the Thinking Skill of Analysis and Synthesis Important?

There are numerous reasons why we use analysis and synthesis. Complex problems are more easily solved by breaking them up then solving them one step at a time. For example, a story problem in mathematics needs to be decoded into the substeps before it can be solved. Knowledge about the individual pieces and how they relate and integrate provides insight into how to construct the whole. For example, a mechanic can repair a car only by understanding how each part functions and how the parts fit together. Overgeneralized perception, which is an inability to see the parts in the context of the whole, leads to errors in thinking. An example of overgeneralized perception is when an individual's behavior is confused with and ascribed to a group or to cultural characteristics.

When and Where Is the Thinking Skill of Analysis and Synthesis Used?

There are numerous contexts where we use analysis and synthesis. At times, it is necessary to identify a single part in a whole, for example finding the relevant paragraph in a story, looking up a telephone number in the directory, or finding a street on a map. In other situations, adding all the parts to make a whole is required, for example following a cookie recipe, knitting squares to make a patchwork quilt, or assembling a puzzle. Understanding the relationship between the parts and the whole is essential, for example, in identifying the sound made by each instrument in an orchestra and seeing how the instruments combine to create euphony; understanding how each piece of litter contributes to environmental pollution; realizing how each individual vote adds up to majority rule in a government body.

Cognitive Conundrum—Analysis and Synthesis

There is a term sometimes used in business circles: *analysis paralysis*. It refers to a situation where we get so bogged down in minutiae that we fail to see the critical big picture. What do you think?

BRIDGING ANALYSIS AND SYNTHESIS TO FORMAL LEARNING CONTEXTS

Numerous formal learning experiences can be used to mediate analysis and synthesis.

Humanities

- Show how playwrights select and sequence individual scenes in a chosen play.
- Analyze language according to figures of speech (e.g., onomatopoeia, alliteration), and show how they contribute to the synthesis of meaning.
- Appreciate poetry through analyzing verse (e.g., rhythm, theme, mood, tone).

Social Sciences

- Show how social events can be described in terms of a composite of different dimensions (e.g., economic, political, cultural).
- Consider the environment in terms of all the key elements that comprise it—communities, buildings, vegetation, facilities, and so on.

Sciences

- Identify substances by labeling their various components (e.g., H_2O is two parts hydrogen and one part oxygen). Show how synthesis in chemistry can change the properties of the resulting substance.
- Analyze soil composition to identify the variety of minerals that make up a sample.
- Review research done on genomes, genetic engineering, and analysis of DNA and its impact on the human species.
- Identify the series of operations needed to solve complex mathematical and scientific problems.

Arts

- Note how the color wheel is built up with various color combinations (i.e., primary colors create secondary colors).
- Analyze works of art according to stylistic criteria such as form, color, line, tone, and so on. Show how the synthesis of such has resulted in recognizable periods and artists in history.

Technology

- Choose a manufacturing concern and analyze how the various machines, processes, and functions interact to produce an entirely new product.
- Design a website for yourself, and work out what essential components you would like to include—blogs, hyperlinks, video lines, and so on.

BRIDGING ANALYSIS AND SYNTHESIS TO INFORMAL LEARNING CONTEXTS

General

- Assist students in reading difficult words by breaking them down into syllables or phonic sounds.
- Analyze essay or test questions carefully to ensure clear understanding.
- Show how synthesis of discrete parts can create a valuable whole (e.g., jigsaw pieces, ingredients in a cake, tangrams).

Health and Personal Development

- Review ways in which complex health problems can be broken down into manageable parts for healing and resolution (e.g., eating disorders—nutrition review, calorie counts, exercise routines, weekly weigh-ins, counseling).

Home

- Provide opportunities for children to create a whole from its parts by assembling building blocks, Legos, Brio mechanical toys, or puzzles. Play games that involve combining parts to make wholes (e.g., Scrabble, puzzles).
- Build a collage of feelings in the form of a blanket of fabric or paper that can be hung up on the wall and shared with others in the family.
- Invite children to observe the different rules and moves that are played in a team game.

Community

- Explore all the factors associated with an established system. For example, when integrating new members into an established team, how will the new "parts" affect the existing whole?

Multicultural

- Analyze the customs and values of various cultures. Discussing the following traditional customs:
  - Eating certain foods with one's hands instead of with eating utensils
  - Having elderly family members live with their children's families
  - Placing more importance on female members of the society or family unit
  - Marrying someone selected by the family
- Which would you like to include in your "ideal" society?

APPLICATION OF ANALYSIS AND SYNTHESIS—THINK GLOBAL, ACT LOCAL

The skills involved in analysis and synthesis can be applied in the community setting. For example, consider a group of people in the community discussing ways to reduce their carbon footprint.

The strategy of *thinking globally, acting locally* implies seeing a problem in its macro sense (synthesis)—global warming and carbon emissions—but dealing with the component parts in a structured micro sense (analysis). In the community, we can work on ways to reduce our own carbon footprint (e.g., cycling to work, small scale carbon trading schemes, planting new trees, using electric or hybrid cars).

FEUERSTEIN'S THEORY IN MEDIATING ANALYSIS AND SYNTHESIS

Feuerstein's (1980) theory focuses on three areas that impact the development of the thinking skills. These include the *mediated learning experience* (MLE)—the type of interaction initiated by a mediator; the *cognitive functions*—the thinking skills of the learner; and the *cognitive map*—an analysis of the learning task. These three areas provide techniques for analyzing the interaction between the mediator, the learner, and the learning task. They provide a useful framework to use when mediating the thinking skill of *analysis and synthesis.* This can be illustrated using the example of essay writing.

Mediated Learning Experience

Feuerstein's (1980) 12 criteria of MLE (see Appendix A) provide the mediator with techniques that help mediate the skill of analysis and synthesis when essay writing. Mediating *meaning* will give the learner an understanding of the intrinsic purpose or reason behind analyzing an essay into its component parts of introduction, body, and conclusion and thus an emotional investment in reconstructing these parts into a cohesive whole.

Cognitive Functions

The list of cognitive functions (see Appendix B) at the input, elaboration, and output phases give a framework for targeting specific skills needed to ensure effective essay writing. This involves, for example, breaking the content into its components parts and sequencing these in order to create a meaningful flow (*understanding of temporal concepts at the input phase*); linking cause and effect so that the essay is well supported and justified (*meaningful grasp of reality at the elaboration phase*); and using appropriate and descriptive language so that the reader can comprehend the final product (*adequate expressive verbal tools at the output phase*).

Cognitive Map

The cognitive map can be used to analyze and manipulate the learning task to ensure that it is pitched at a meaningful and useful level for the learner (see Appendix C). In this example, essay writing is a standard academic task (*content*), requiring competence with reading and writing (*written modality*), where the structure or format becomes more familiar and less complicated with practice (*decreasing levels of abstraction, novelty, and complexity*).

Thus, the techniques of MLE, the cognitive functions and cognitive map can be used to mediate the skill of *analysis and synthesis* in essay writing.

WINDOW TO INTERNATIONAL
RESEARCH ON COGNITIVE EDUCATION

Analytic Perception is the sixth instrument used in Feuerstein's (1980) Instrumental Enrichment (IE) program. Overall, there are 14 instruments that make up the IE program, which has been implemented in a range of contexts internationally. This extract describes research done using IE with children with learning disabilities and socioemotional problems in Belgium:

> Schnitzer, Andries, and Lebeer (2007) investigated the kind of intervention that would be effective in modifying cognitive as well as socioemotional behavior, and at the same time focused on contextual interaction and intervention. The study was carried out in Belgium with 11- to 13-year-old students with learning disabilities and behavior problems in special schools. After receiving 14 sessions of IE, the children showed a marked increase in certain cognitive functions (including hypothetical thinking, and the perception and understanding of humor). A significant effect on socioemotional behavior could not be shown quantitatively but was evident qualitatively, in interviews. The mediating attitude of the teachers was a key influencing factor in producing lasting changes. The authors conclude that, provided they approach children as well as teachers in a holistic way, focusing on cognitive as well as socioemotional behavioral changes, programs such as IE may become powerful instruments to help children as well as teachers in a highly differentiated, inclusive school environment.

"The whole is greater than the sum of its parts."

—Aristotle

"Whenever two people meet there are really six people present. There is each man as he sees himself, each man as the other person sees him, each man as he really is."

—William James

"Culture is the sum of all forms of art, of love, and of thought, which, in the course of centuries, have enabled man to be less enslaved."

—Andre Malraux

7

Problem Solving

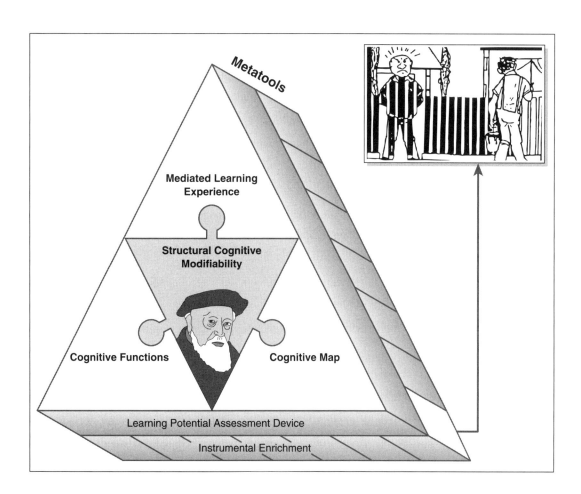

The thinking skill that is outlined in this chapter is *problem solving.* This involves identifying that something has gone wrong, analyzing why it has gone wrong, and finding solutions to make it right. When something goes wrong, there is a sense of disequilibrium that alerts us to a problem. Restoring equilibrium to a system is when the problem is solved. This thinking skill involves identifying causes of problems, consequences of actions, solutions to problems, consequences of solutions, as well as moral and ethical behavior.

The thinking skill of problem solving is taught in the *illustrations instrument* of Feuerstein's (1980) Instrumental Enrichment (IE) program. Feuerstein uses illustrations or cartoons to show in a humorous way why problems occur and different ways of understanding and solving them. The symbol for this instrument is an illustration of a man who is mechanically painting a wall without thinking and so paints over another man who, also failing to think, gets painted. This illustrates in an absurd way the problem is related to doing a job without thinking. In the illustrations instrument many humorous situations—often exaggerated and absurd—are depicted as springboards to discussing problems and how to solve them.

PROBLEM SOLVING—WHAT, WHY, WHEN, AND WHERE?

Why do problems arise? Can all problems be solved directly? When does one need to use creative and ingenious solutions to problems? What can we learn from absurd or humorous situations? What values govern the solutions we choose in solving problems?

The ability to answer these kinds of questions depends on the ability to perceive that disequilibrium exists—that a problem has been identified. Once a problem has been identified, it is necessary to restore equilibrium—provide an appropriate solution to the problem. The ability to problem solve covers a range of different cognitive skills. It involves understanding cause-and-effect relationships; for example, understanding that if I act impulsively, I may cause an accident to happen. It also involves being creative in solving difficult dilemmas; for example, many of the most threatening world problems, such as global warming and poverty, need solutions that haven't been identified yet. At a more intrapersonal level, problem solving involves examining our motives for the solutions we choose; for example, how to resolve a marital conflicts and so on.

What Is the Thinking Skill of Problem Solving?

Problem solving involves identifying cause-and-effect relationships. It begins with identifying that something is wrong and then either learning from the situation or solving it. It involves interpreting life events, making moral judgments, and acting in an innovative and ingenious way. Through problem solving, we gain insight into our values and creative potential—we learn from life. Many problems have a similar underlying cause (e.g., carelessness, impulsivity, not following instructions, egocentrism, misunderstanding, imprecision, conflicting values or views). The solutions to one problem can often be generalized to solve another, and so the underlying causes and effects need to be transcended beyond the specific example.

Why Is the Thinking Skill of Problem Solving Important?

There are many reasons for teaching the skill of problem solving—in educational settings as well as in everyday life situations. In the illustrations instrument, this is done through humorous cartoons or situations. Often, the best way to learn from a mistake or problem is to laugh at it. We learn through laughing at mishaps. Feuerstein (1980) recognized this in the following illustrations of problem scenarios:

- A man who, irritated by a hornet, impulsively swats the nest, which results in him being chased by a swarm of hornets. This humorous scenario suggests that anger and resulting impulsivity is often not the best way to solve a problem.

- Two yoked donkeys pull stubbornly in opposite directions against each other so that neither is able to eat corn bundles just next to each of them. They realize eventually that working with each other rather than pulling against each will result in them being able to reach both bundles in turn. This illustrates an underlying solution to some of life's more complicated problems—that cooperation (rather than competition) is often the best way to achieve a common goal.

When and Where Is the Thinking Skill of Problem Solving Used?

There are numerous contexts and situations where problem solving occurs. In decision-making, we need to problem solve to act according to our value system—for example whether to cheat or study for a test. In everyday life situations, we solve problems in both direct and indirect ways. Direct, straightforward problem solving might involve sorting out a confusion in communication by rephrasing a comment. Indirect and creative problem solving might involve using a nylon stocking as a makeshift fan belt to get a car to the repair shop.

Cognitive Conundrum—Problem Solving

It has been said that the "Z generation" are being born with "a mouse in one hand and a mobile phone in the other." They expect instant gratification and their problems to be solved with immediacy and often by technology.

Will this change their fundamental ability to problem solve or perceive disequilibrium in situations? What do you think?

BRIDGING PROBLEM SOLVING TO FORMAL LEARNING CONTEXTS

Numerous formal learning experiences can be used to mediate problem solving.

Humanities

- Use debate as a means of finding solutions to a problem (e.g., support or defend a point of view during an argument).
- Use examples in literature to evaluate problematic situations (e.g., the family feud in Shakespeare's *Romeo and Juliet,* Red Riding Hood's meeting with "Grandmother").

Social Sciences

- Create scenarios to explore historical issues (e.g., pretending you are Albert Schweitzer solving the problems of malaria in Africa in the last century).
- Use historical and contemporary newspaper cartoons to interpret political and social problems.
- Encourage students to solve environmental problems creatively (e.g., soil erosion, deforestation, oil spills in the ocean, whaling, global warming).
- Critically evaluate existing policies that control environmental problems in terms of short-term and long-term effects (e.g., protecting endangered species, water conservation, protecting the rain forest to prevent depletion of the ozone layer in the atmosphere).

Sciences

- Outline and discuss the steps involved in performing a science experiment to test a hypothesis (e.g., testing acidity or basicity of water to ensure that it is safe for crops).
- Encourage divergent thinking in solving technological problems in supplying energy needs (e.g., wind, solar, battery-powered engines, rain water tanks, energy-efficient appliances, electric cars).
- Encourage individual approaches in solving math problems (e.g., asking how many ways you can get to the sum of 45).

Arts

- Work through all the problem-solving steps in producing a play (e.g., props, costumes, music, script, lighting, staging, casting the characters).

Technology

- Examine how Internet chat rooms, listservs, and so on have impacted communication, and analyze ways in which they are used to help solve various problems.
- Contrast new technologies (e.g., broadband, Internet access, fax transmission, PDAs, mobile phones, satellite TV) with those of times gone by, and discuss how they have helped overcome a multitude of problems in communication.

BRIDGING PROBLEM SOLVING TO INFORMAL LEARNING CONTEXTS

General

- Appreciate that what might be a problem to one person may not a problem to another (e.g., for some teachers, a noisy classroom is a learning classroom; for others it is a disruptive environment).
- Encourage independent, divergent, and autonomous solutions to problems (e.g., math problems, teacher-student conflict, writing or spelling difficulties, boredom).

Health and Personal Development

- Develop an awareness of cause-and-effect situations in society (e.g., the consequences of drug and alcohol abuse, not using contraceptives, aggressive and antisocial behavior).
- Illustrate the importance of being prepared and being able to improvise in problem solving (e.g., having a job interview suddenly scheduled during a time when you'll be on a vacation).
- Examine personal strategies that can be used to solve physical and emotional problems (e.g., relaxation, exercise, time out).

Home

- Refer to the illustrations student instrument, to the cartoon of two yoked donkeys pulling a cart in different directions. Show how such a cartoon can teach the concept of cooperation as a means of problem solving. This illustration can be bridged to demonstrate to children the need for cooperation in order to play a team game successfully.
- Through the cartoon of the mother dog and her puppies in the illustrations student instrument, we can demonstrate how individuality exists in a family. Discuss the different ways one copes when faced with a problem.
- Mediate seeing the funny side of situations in the home, such as in being able to laugh at oneself to release tension and to solve or prevent problems from being blown out of proportion.
- Help make safe decisions in emergencies in the home. Impulsive solutions could exacerbate the situation (e.g., pouring water on a oil fire on the stove).
- Use problem-solving skills as springboards to creative activities involving lateral and divergent thinking to achieve positive outcomes (e.g., finding a creative way to alleviate teenage binge drinking—graphic messages on alcohol labels?).

APPLICATION OF PROBLEM SOLVING— CYBER BULLIES AND SUICIDE SCRIPTS

The skills involved in problem solving can be applied in the school and home settings. For example, consider the ever-expanding problem of children and adolescents being bullied and emotionally abused through Internet sites and text messages.

Whilst technology has made our lives richer, it can come at a cost. It has been responsible for making some of our disenfranchised youth more isolated and disconnected through cyber-bullying. Cyber-bullying is a ubiquitous and destructive type of emotional harassment carried out through e-mails, chat rooms, text messaging, blogs, and so on. Problem solving for this behavior involves three major actions by teachers and parents: (1) Supervise—stay in touch by discussing Internet issues with children, and note any behavior changes related to online activity; (2) Educate— teach students to tell someone when they are being bullied. Youth need to know who to contact when cyber–bullying is evident, and adults need to be aware of the procedure for removing distressing information from the internet; (3) Equip—use filter functions, block chat or peer-to-peer messaging, block Internet applications such as VOIP, chat rooms, games, and so on. These actions can alleviate the problem and minimize the potential harm.

FEUERSTEIN'S THEORY IN MEDIATING PROBLEM SOLVING

Feuerstein's (1980) theory focuses on three areas that impact the development of the thinking skills. These include the *mediated learning experience* (MLE)—the type of interaction initiated by a mediator; the *cognitive functions*—the thinking skills of the learner; and the *cognitive map*—an analysis of the learning task. These three areas provide techniques for analyzing the interaction between the mediator, the learner, and the learning task. They provide a useful framework to use when mediating the thinking skill of *problem solving*. This can be illustrated using the example of a science experiment.

Mediated Learning Experience

Feuerstein's (1980) criteria of MLE (see Appendix A) provide the mediator with techniques that help mediate the skill of problem solving when testing out hypotheses in a science experiment. For example *self-regulation and control of behavior* will help the learner be aware of the need to adjust his or her behavior depending on the outcome of the experiment. This links to taking responsibility for his or her actions in all stages of the experiment. Mediating the *search for the optimistic alternative* will instill in the learner an open and nonjudgmental attitude to the outcome of the experiment and the expectation that a solution will be achieved.

Cognitive Functions

The list of cognitive functions (see Appendix B) at the input, elaboration, and output phases give a framework for targeting specific skills needed to ensure a science experiment is effectively carried out. For example, mediating statements such as "What are the instructions?" "What stayed the same, and what changed?" "What are all the elements involved?" will guard against impulsive data gathering (*ability to conserve constancies and capacity to consider more than one source of information at the input phase*). Results of the experiment can be used to formulate a general rule to apply in other problem situations (*inferential hypothesis testing at the elaboration phase*). Finally, a mature and clear output response is needed (*worked through output phase*).

Cognitive Map

The cognitive map can be used to analyze and manipulate the learning task to ensure that it is pitched at a meaningful and useful level for the learner (see Appendix C). In this example, conducting a science experiment is a complex practical task (*content*) requiring skill in working with scientific equipment (*physical modality*) to test hypotheses and draw abstract conclusions from the concrete example (*linking concrete to abstract, high level of novelty and complexity*).

Thus, the techniques of MLE, the cognitive functions and cognitive map can be used to mediate the skill of *problem solving* in a science experiment.

WINDOW TO INTERNATIONAL
RESEARCH ON COGNITIVE EDUCATION

Illustrations is the seventh instrument used in Feuerstein's (1980) Instrumental Enrichment (IE) program. Overall, there are 14 instruments that make up the IE program which, has been implemented in a range of contexts internationally. This extract describes research done using IE with children who have dyslexia and reading problems in Spain:

Sanchez (1991) matched 25 and 22 students from a rural school in Spain in an experimental (E) and control (C) group, respectively, on such parameters as age, IQ, and socioeconomic status. They had low scores on a language test that measured spoken and written vocabulary, and grammar skills. The E group was given three hours of IE per week for a period of three years, using the following IE instruments:

organization of dots, orientation in space I, comparisons, analytic perception, categorization, temporal relations, and instructions. In addition to these instruments, the author designed special materials, facilitating the transfer of IE tasks to language. At the end of the three-year period, students were posttested on the intelligence and language tests. The E group improved significantly more than the C group on measures of verbal and intellectual functioning. Thus, greater improvement was shown for E in all areas of the language test, but particularly in vocabulary and grammar. Further, the E group scored significantly higher on verbal IQ and on the vocabulary, comprehension, and similarities subtests of the Wechsler Intelligence Scale for Children.

> *"True genius resides in the capacity for evaluation of uncertain, hazardous, and conflicting information."*
>
> —Winston Churchill

8

Relationships

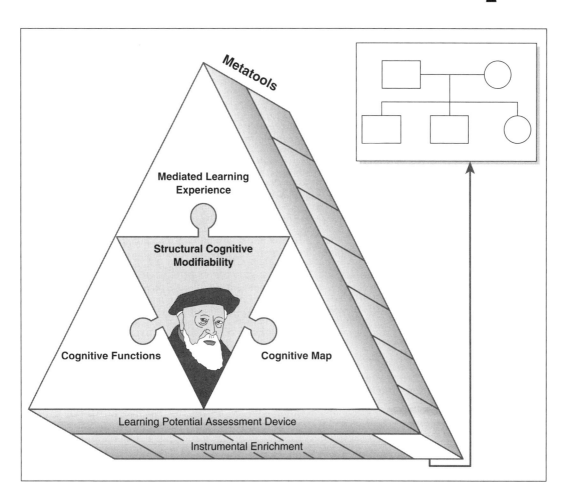

The thinking skill that is outlined in this chapter concerns *relationships*. This focuses on inferring, understanding, and explaining the connection between two or more people or groups and their involvement with each other. This thinking skill looks primarily at the way in which people are related by birth or marriage—and is bridged to other forms of relationships, involving networks, systems, or other connections.

The thinking skill of Relationships is taught in the *family relations instrument* of Feuerstein's (1980) Instrumental Enrichment (IE) program. Feuerstein's symbol for this instrument is a genealogical map or genogram that illustrates the relationships among members of a nuclear family. The squares represent males and the circles, females. This genogram describes the relationships of marriage (husband and wife) and parenthood (two sons and a daughter).

RELATIONSHIPS—WHAT, WHY, WHEN, AND WHERE?

Are all relationships permanent? Can an individual have a number of different relationships at the same time? Do relationships determine roles?

The ability to answer these kinds of questions depends on the ability to understand and project relationships. A relationship is a connection, tie, or bond between two or more objects or people. There are many different types of relationships, and an understanding of these makes us more aware of interpersonal, institutional, and societal dynamics. Being related or having a connection or association can be due to marriage, birth, kinship, or membership.

What Is the Thinking Skill of Relationships?

A relationship is a certain kind of link between separate entities. The family relations instrument describes various kinds of links or connections. These include relationships by law (e.g., husband and wife); relationships by blood (e.g., parent and child); relationships that are permanent (e.g., sisters and brothers); and relationships that are transient (e.g., divorcees). These terms define familiar relationships and the different connections between family members. The concept of relationship or connections between people can be extended to include memberships beyond familial boundaries. This could include relationships and membership within a work context (e.g., manager and employee), in a school context (e.g., teacher, principal, and student), recreational or interest relationships (e.g., coach and players in a sport's team or members of choir), community and group relationships (e.g., membership within a cultural or religious group), as well as digital relationships or online interest group (e.g., "friends" in a Facebook or other social networking site).

Why Is the Thinking Skill of Relationships Important?

There are many reasons for teaching the skill of relationships. Focusing on the connection between people develops an appreciation of the different kinds of relationships that exist, for example direct (e.g., a marriage) versus indirect (e.g., sister-in-law); and horizontal (e.g., husband-wife) versus hierarchical (e.g., parent-child). Examination of these relationships suggests that the descriptions could vary depending on the specific context and power relationship, with a hierarchical relationship becoming horizontal and vice versa. It is also important to understand the multiplicity of relationships an individual can have at any given time (e.g., a woman can be a mother, daughter, and wife at the same time) and to follow the progression of relationships and realize they are not static (e.g., a mother may become a mother-in-law). Relationships extend to all systems (e.g., school, society), and the kinds of connections operating within them provide a basis for making inferences, drawing appropriate conclusions, and making comparisons between various systems

When and Where Is the Thinking Skill of Relationships Used?

There are numerous contexts and situations where relationships occur. In this chapter, there is a focus on differentiating between various kinds of relationships in a range of family situations. This begins with the familial relationships of a (Western) nuclear family, but can extend from there to include the extended family and the family of nations. Different cultures and contexts define the relationships between family members in different ways—for example polygamy, where a person has more than one spouse, is practiced in some cultures but is considered a crime in other cultures. Relationships can be further discussed in other areas, for example the genealogy of animals, the family of nouns, and the connections that occur in work, social, or interest groups. Identity within a family, group, community, or culture will differ and as a result, so too will the kind of connection or network that one has both within and between people in those groups and subgroups.

Cognitive Conundrum—Relationships

In mediating the skills of establishing relationships, is there a danger that we begin to view the world in terms of rigid and set connections? Is there a place for appreciating the unique and unconnected elements of an object or situation? What do you think?

BRIDGING RELATIONSHIPS TO FORMAL LEARNING CONTEXTS

Numerous formal learning experiences can be used to mediate relationships.

Humanities

- Identify word families that have a common cluster of letters representing a sound (e.g., *tch, sh, ae*).
- Discuss vocabulary used to identify different family relations (e.g., *son, grandmother, husband, great uncle, father*).
- Analyze different types of relationships in literature (e.g., Romeo and Juliet, Anthony and Cleopatra, Oliver Twist and Fagan, Dorothy and the Tin Man).

Social Sciences

- Illustrate the hierarchical relationships in governments or governing bodies by using a genogram structure.
- Discuss different types of dynasties and royal families (e.g., the Ming dynasty, the Swazi royal family, the Tudors).
- Discuss the types of relationships that exist among countries (e.g., those that belong to the British Commonwealth, those linked to the EEC).

Sciences

- Discuss the position of planets and stars in the solar systems and their relationship to the different suns.
- Examine different relationships in the animal kingdom (e.g., ants in a social colony, bees in a hive, doves mating for life).
- Show how different relationships can be illustrated in mathematics (e.g., $2 + 4 = 4 + 2$, $A > B > C$ or $C < B < A$).

Arts

- Examine various symbols that have been used to represent gender and relationships in art.
- Critique various art forms in terms of the techniques used to create relationships (e.g., between positive and negative space, between different colors and hues, between foreground and background).

Technology

- Research the connections between various technologies (e.g., lasers and keyhole surgery, MRI and cancer treatments, fiber optics and communication devices, broadband and computers).
- Discuss how the Internet allows for a relationship between computer networks across the world.

BRIDGING RELATIONSHIPS TO FORMAL LEARNING CONTEXTS

General

- Play games, such as chess, that illustrate the relationship between different players and places (e.g., in chess, the queen is more powerful than the bishop, and the pawns are equal).
- Outline a typical school hierarchy (e.g., principal, teachers, teacher aides, students), and identify relationships and roles.
- Discuss different types of interpersonal relationships (e.g., peer-peer, teacher-student, husband-wife).

Health and Personal Development

- Encourage students to evaluate the relationships they have with family members and friends. Discuss what they gain from these interactions and what they give to the friendships.
- Help foster an appreciation of different cultural structures by researching the family relationships and function of members within the existing culture.

Home

- Design a family tree by cutting up photographs and pasting them on a chart to illustrate the relationships among family members.
- Use various techniques with young children to work through relationship problems with family members (e.g., accepting a new baby, introducing a step parent, sibling rivalry).

Counseling

- Develop an understanding of the roles and responsibilities of family members by examining the relationships between them.
- Examine institutions by identifying the roles and relationships of their members, discussing how changes in them can bring about improvement in interaction, functioning, achievement, cooperation, and satisfaction.

APPLICATION OF RELATIONSHIPS— RELATIVES AND RELATIONS

Skills involved in the study of relationships can be applied in community setting. For example, consider a scenario of various individuals—baby, grandfather, toddler, mother, and so on interacting with each other in a blended family environment.

Statistics reveal that an average of one in five children has a stepparent or step-family. Family structures are no longer fixed in a nuclear framework. They can be dynamic and complex—blended, step, adopted, foster, extended, tribal, de facto, single parent, same-sex, and so on.

In view of this, it is important that we, as a community, establish support systems and infrastructures that recognize these dynamics. Education and acceptance of the diverse nature of family structures allows communities to grow without conflict and prejudice. Our efforts need to be focused particularly on children who need to feel that they are part of a family unit, even though it may constantly be changing.

FEUERSTEIN'S THEORY IN MEDIATING RELATIONSHIPS

Feuerstein's (1980) theory focuses on three areas that impact the development of the thinking skills. These include the *mediated learning experience* (MLE)—the type of interaction initiated by a mediator; the *cognitive functions*—the thinking skills of the learner; and the *cognitive map*—an analysis of the learning task. These three areas provide techniques for analyzing the interaction between the mediator, the learner, and the learning task. They provide a useful framework to use when mediating the thinking skill of *relationships.* This can be illustrated using the example of a Punnett square to work out the dominant and recessive alleles (genetic coding) for inherited characteristics in families.

Mediated Learning Experience

Feuerstein's (1980) criteria of MLE (see Appendix A) provide the mediator with techniques that help mediate the skill of relationships—for example, using a Punnett square, where the genetic characteristics passed to the next generation in a family is determined. In mediating *a sense of belonging* the mediator can instill in the learner an appreciation of being part of family, knowing where and how people fit in at a biological and psychological level. Mediating *a sense of self-change* reinforces for the learner the dynamic nature of relationships and how families, cultures, and communities are open to modifiability over generations.

Cognitive Functions

The list of cognitive functions (see Appendix B) at the input, elaboration, and output phases give a framework for targeting specific skills needed to determine the dominant and recessive alleles (genetic coding). It would be important to focus the learner on entering the information into the Punnett square in a clear, systematic, and precise manner (*systematic exploration of a learning situation and capacity to consider more than one source of information at the input phase*), see the connections between the dominant and recessive alleles (*project virtual relationships at the elaboration phase*), and be precise in formulating a response (*precise and accurate data at the output phase*).

Cognitive Map

The cognitive map can be used to analyze and manipulate the learning task to ensure that it is pitched at a meaningful and useful level for the learner (see Appendix C). In this example, determining genetic inheritance is an involved biological activity (*content*) requiring skill in using Punnett calculations (*symbolic and figural modality*) to draw conclusions about dominant genes (*high levels of abstraction, novelty, and complexity*).

Thus, the techniques of MLE, the cognitive functions, and cognitive map can be used to mediate the skill of *relationships,* using the example of a Punnett square to work out the dominant and recessive alleles (genetic coding) for inherited characteristics in families.

WINDOW TO INTERNATIONAL RESEARCH ON COGNITIVE EDUCATION

Family Relations is the eighth instrument used in Feuerstein's (1980) Instrumental Enrichment (IE) program. Overall, there are 14 instruments that make up the IE program, which has been implemented in a range of contexts internationally. This extract describes research done using IE with people in Israel who are blind.

The IE materials were adapted for use by blind and partially sighted students. Various techniques were used to translate the materials into Braille text and other tactile means of appreciating the materials. Gouzman (1997) reported on a series of studies in Israel with the blind. The program has been used with primary and secondary school students, integrated into regular schools, in a special school for the blind, with young adults in a preparatory university course, and with elderly, new immigrants in an intensive Hebrew program. Outcomes of the program implementation include changes in the behaviors, cognition, and self-image of blind learners. In the field of behavior, students have demonstrated greater alertness and involvement in the lessons. The self-image of the blind learners has improved significantly, with students setting for themselves much higher educational and employment goals. Cognitively, a significant change occurred with the blind learners acquiring "quasi-visual" representation of objects and processes, learning to use schematic representations and models, developing learning strategies, and expanding the areas of their cognitive functioning.

"Family faces are magic mirrors. Looking at people who belong to us, we see the past, present and future. We make discoveries about ourselves."

—Gail Lumet Buckley

9

Temporal
Concepts

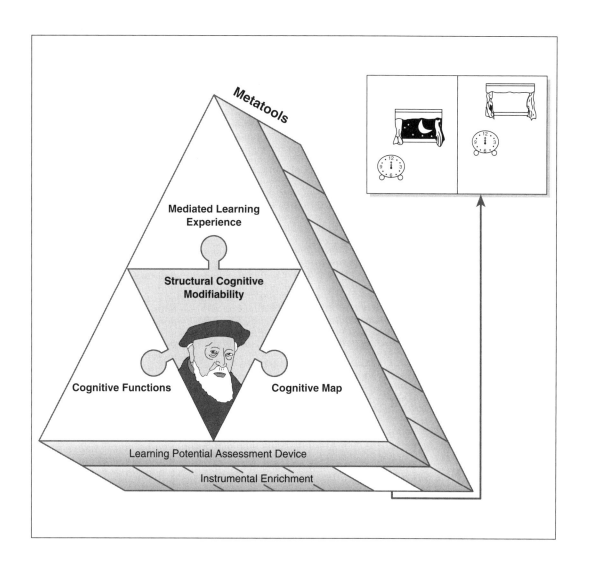

The thinking skill that is outlined in this chapter is that of *temporal concepts*. This involves having an understanding of the concept of time. Common definitions of *time* include "a prescribed or allotted period," "the interval between events," and "a moment at which something takes place." Time, in Western society, is usually characterized as consisting of past, present, and future. *To time* means "to measure or record the duration, speed, or rate of something," or "to regulate or to keep to a rhythm or beat."

The thinking skill relating to time concepts is taught in the temporal relations instrument of Feuerstein's (1980) Instrumental Enrichment (IE) program. Feuerstein's symbol for the instrument is a comparison of two aspects of time—natural time and constructed time. Natural time is represented as day and night (moonlight or sunlight as seen through the window), and constructed time is represented by the clock (12 o'clock midnight and 12 o'clock noon). Both sources of information are needed to tell the time.

TEMPORAL CONCEPTS—
WHAT, WHY, WHEN, AND WHERE?

> *"Procrastination is the thief of time." "Time is money."*
>
> *"Time heals all wounds." "How time flies."*
>
> *"Do not squander time, for that is the stuff that life is made of."*

Appreciating these quotations depends on the ability to understand concepts of time. Time is one of the most abstract concepts and can be described in a number of different ways—calendars (time as constructed by humans) or cycles of the moon (natural time). Managing time is one of the keys to effective living.

What Are the Thinking Skills
Related to Temporal Concepts?

Temporal relations involves understanding concepts of time—both natural and created. For example, natural time includes the seasons of the year, the days and nights, rhythms of sleep, a heartbeat, a pulse, and so on. Natural time is approximate and relative. For instance, different people feel hungry or tired at different times of the day; heartbeats follow different rhythms depending on whether one is anxious, relaxed, or active; the sun sets at different times depending on geographical area. In contrast, time that is constructed by humans use devices such as clocks, calendars, and hourglasses. Constructed time is absolute and accurate (e.g., one hour equals 60 minutes), but dependent on culture (e.g., the Jewish calendar year differs from both the Roman and Chinese calendars).

Why Are the Thinking Skills
of Temporal Concepts Important?

There are many reasons for teaching the skill of temporal concepts. These include an appreciation of how the past influences the present and how both past and present impact the future. Being able to manage time effectively is important, and this involves planning ahead—working out short- and long-term goals. Managing time also involves following a sequence of events from beginning to end, anticipating consequences of actions (e.g., what will happen next if I do this now?), and delaying gratification (e.g., restraining certain behavior until an appropriate time).

When and Where Are the Thinking skills of Temporal Concepts Used?

There are numerous contexts and situations where temporal concepts are used and necessary. These include the home context (e.g., routines of eating and sleeping), at school (e.g., following the school schedules or timetables and meeting deadlines), in the community (e.g., planning long-term projects), and they are necessary in order to function efficiently in life (e.g., planning ahead, learning from past experiences, following a sequence).

Different religions and cultures structure time in different ways. For example, in the Judeo-Christian approach, time is linear, beginning with the act of creation by God. God is eternal and exists in eternity, out of time. In other religions and cultures, such as certain Native American groups, Hinduism, and Buddhism, time is cyclical, where there are repeated cycles of creation. The Aboriginal people in Australia believe in two forms of time—the daily objective activity, and infinite spiritual cycle called the "dreamtime." Other cultures, such as certain groups in Africa, believe in a connection to their ancestors in spiritual time.

Time is also interpreted differently depending on one's psychological state. Different individuals may judge an identical length of time to be passing at different rates depending on whether they are having fun or under stress, participating or waiting, and so on. Time is said "to fly" or "to drag" depending on one's state of mind. In this way, time is linked to the Einsteinian notion of relativity. Hallucinogenic drugs can also alter one's perception of time—which may appear to slow down, stop, speed up, go backwards, and even seem out of sequence.

Time measurement and time management are two central dimensions of temporal concepts. Measuring time has been a core theme throughout civilization, and different tools and techniques have been used, including the sun's movements, the phases of the moon, the swing of a pendulum, clocks, and calendars. Time management involves the cognitive and life skill of ordering and structuring events into sequences. As technology improves, tools such as e-mail, the Internet, faxes, instant messaging, and so on seem to speed up the time it takes to complete tasks, creating more challenges for time management.

Cognitive Conundrum—Temporal Concepts

The concept of "slow learning" has been raised by those involved in education. It has been proposed that slowing down the learning pace will improve the quality and depth of knowledge gained as opposed to the "surface" or superficial breadth of "fast" learning. Slow learning will also preserve mental health, reduce stress, and lead to greater introspection. What do you think?

BRIDGING TEMPORAL CONCEPTS TO FORMAL LEARNING CONTEXTS

Numerous formal learning experiences can be used to mediate temporal concepts.

Humanities

- Discuss and sequence classic novels according to periods in time.
- Examine the grammatical structure and vocabulary used for indicating past, present, and future tenses (e.g., *was, am, will be*).
- Imagine you are in a time machine and can travel through time, in effect turning the clock backwards or forwards. Write a creative story.

Social Sciences

- Draw up timelines to illustrate different events and periods in time (e.g., Ice Age, Stone Age, Dark Ages).
- Review how events of the past (e.g., abolition of slavery, fall of the Berlin Wall, the Bali Bombing) have impacted current political practices in society.

Sciences

- Illustrate life cycles and seasons in the plant and animal kingdoms. For example, study the cyclical nature of metamorphosis (e.g., egg, caterpillar, cocoon, butterfly).
- Solve problems in physics that use equations involving time (e.g., time = distance/speed; velocity = displacement/time; acceleration = velocity/time).
- Compare representations of digital and analog time (e.g., 4:55 = five minutes to five o'clock).
- Research the various devices used to measure time over the ages (e.g., a burning candle, shadow stick, an egg timer).

Arts

- Identify the paintings and sculpture of artists throughout the centuries and the ways in which we appreciate them today.
- Explain the sequence and timing involved in printing processes (e.g., developing photographs or offset printing).
- Highlight the importance of tempo, beat, and rhythm in musical compositions and dance.

Technology

- Discuss how our use of words regarding timeframes has had to change with the invention of new technologies (e.g., microseconds, nanoseconds) in neutron physics and medical sciences.
- Examine ways in which processes can be accelerated without the loss of quality (e.g., using robotic cutters instead of the human hand, using computer software to direct an operation).

BRIDGING TEMPORAL CONCEPTS TO INFORMAL LEARNING CONTEXTS

General

- Draw up a school calendar depicting the events of the year (e.g., homecoming, football game, prom).
- Help students structure a study timetable for major examinations.
- Explore the concept of "personal time" (e.g., having time out in a conflict situation).
- Help solve personal problems by analyzing whether an individual is "in-step" or "out-of-step" with society (e.g., is the individual living in the past or dwelling on the future?).
- Analyze in what ways students should reflect on the past, but still allow them to move forward with time.
- Help individuals explore the ways in which their behavior has changed over time, and what they are doing now to ensure good health in the future.

Home

- Design timetables for extracurricular activities in picture or graphic form. Display them at home to remind children on which days they need to pack particular supplies to take to school.
- Make sundials or shadow sticks for the garden. Observe how the shade moves at different times of the day. Notice how the sizes of the different shadows change.
- Develop an awareness of time by encouraging the use of watches, diaries, logs, and calendars.
- Teach young children to organize their time (e.g., using the TV guide to plan viewing time around suppertime, homework, bath time, bedtime).
- Make journals, diaries, or scrapbooks of holiday or vacation photos.
- Help in the understanding and appreciation of natural time (e.g., noting phases of the moon, changes in seasons, night and day).
- Create an awareness of biorhythms, body clocks, and other natural rhythms in "physiological" time (e.g., when our bodies tell us it's time to eat or sleep).

Multicultural

- Use the study of time concepts to promote empathy and appreciation of time in different cultures (e.g., siesta time, different days for the Sabbath, four- versus five-day workweeks, summer vacations).
- Explore past, present, and future concepts in various cultures (e.g., the idea of reincarnation, the concept of an afterlife, the philosophy of life being of a circular nature as opposed to a linear one).

APPLICATION OF TEMPORAL CONCEPTS—SLOW AND STEADY

The skills involved in the study of temporal concepts can be applied in the family setting. For example, consider the concept of *slow down*—slow food, slow routes, slow learning, and so on in a home environment.

Studies involving time tend to be focused on how to do things quicker, more efficiently, and more economically. These constructs manifest in all areas of life, from the home to large corporations. In a world where *slow* now has negative connotations, we need to revisit the concept of time. A good place to start is in the family setting where "hurry up" can be replaced with "slow down; take your time," and "fast food" can be replaced with "slow cooking"—a time to savor both the art and the resulting taste. Holidays should involve taking the "slow route," where scenery and culture can be truly appreciated. Perhaps, today it is important that children in classrooms should also be educated in the concept of "slow time" and pausing to reflect.

FEUERSTEIN'S THEORY IN MEDIATING TEMPORAL CONCEPTS

Feuerstein's (1980) theory focuses on three areas that impact the development of the thinking skills. These include the *mediated learning experience* (MLE)—the type of interaction initiated by a mediator; the *cognitive functions*—the thinking skills of the learner; and the *cognitive map*—an analysis of the learning task. These three areas provide techniques for analyzing the interaction between the mediator, the learner, and the learning task. They provide a useful framework to use when mediating the thinking skill of *temporal concepts*. This can be illustrated using the example of planning a study timetable.

Mediated Learning Experience

Feuerstein's (1980) criteria of MLE (see Appendix A) provide the mediator with techniques that help mediate the skill of temporal concepts through planning a study timetable. Mediating *goal planning* will help the learner see the bigger picture of time management and link the study plan to broader career and life goals. Mediating *self regulation and control of behavior* will instill in the learner the understanding that some behaviors might need to change in the short term and that discipline and persistence will be needed in order to actualize the study plan, which will have potentially positive outcomes in the long term.

Cognitive Functions

The list of cognitive functions (see Appendix B) at the input, elaboration, and output phases give a framework for targeting specific skills needed to ensure a sound study timetable is designed. Identifying the essential and nonessential activities and how much time they involve will guard against blurred and sweeping data gathering (*clear exploration of the learning situation at the input phase*). Prioritizing activities and being systematic will result in a sound plan being established (*selecting relevant cues and planning behavior at the elaboration phase*). Finally, overcoming blocking or procrastination will lead to a positive outcome (*worked-through output phase*).

Cognitive Map

The cognitive map can be used to analyze and manipulate the learning task to ensure that it is pitched at a meaningful and useful level for the learner (see Appendix C). In this example, planning a study timetable is a time-management task (*content*) requiring skill in sequencing time onto a time chart (*graphic modality*) to establish a structured time table where content to be studied is aligned with time available to study (*medium levels of abstraction, novelty, and complexity*).

Thus, the techniques of MLE, the cognitive functions, and cognitive map can be used to mediate the skill of *temporal concepts* using a study timetable.

WINDOW TO INTERNATIONAL
RESEARCH ON COGNITIVE EDUCATION

Temporal relations is the ninth instrument used in Feuerstein's (1980) Instrumental Enrichment (IE) program. Overall, there are 14 instruments that make up the IE program, which has been implemented in a range of contexts internationally. This extract describes research done using IE with people in New Zealand who are deaf.

In New Zealand, Thickpenny (1982) found positive results using IE with students who are profoundly deaf when it was used with two classes of adolescent children at a school for the deaf in Auckland. In this study, it was found that the greater the exposure to IE, the wider the use of the cognitive skills. From his research, Thickpenny concluded that IE can be successfully implemented with students who are profoundly deaf, and that it appears to produce generalized application of the cognitive skills learned. Positive results of the use of IE with the deaf were also found by Keane (1983) and Martin (1993) in the United States. Important implications from this research include that the way in which hearing parents mediate the world to their children can be systematically improved, perhaps using the theory of mediated learning as a principle in the construction of any training program. The implications for education are the need to diagnose in children the cognitive deficiencies that are preventing them from achieving acceptable academic levels, and that IE especially adapted for the deaf can be used as a means to their remediation.

> "Whoever doesn't know the past must have little understanding of the present and no vision of the future."
>
> —Joseph S. Raymond

10

Instructions

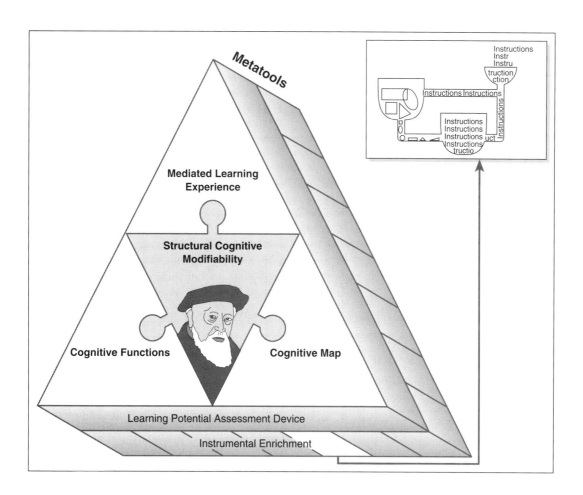

The thinking skill outlined in this chapter is that of *instructions*. Instructions relate to the two reciprocal processes of encoding (giving) and decoding (receiving) information. Instructions are usually encoded using the imperative (using a verb without "to" or any noun or pronoun in front of it). For example, instead of "You should not walk on the grass in this park," the imperative instruction is "Do not walk on the grass." Understanding how to encode or give instructions, and then decode or follow instructions, will save time and energy, and prevent mistakes and errors.

The thinking skill relating to following directions is taught in the *instructions instrument*. Feuerstein's (1980) symbol for instructions is a diagram showing how an instruction involves an input phase (when the instruction is encoded), an elaboration phase (when the instruction is thought about), and an output phase (when the instruction is decoded and carried out). This instrument further illustrates how instructions can consist of either a single directive (e.g., "Do not walk on the grass") or a set of directions to follow (e.g., the steps in baking cookies).

INSTRUCTIONS—WHAT, WHY, WHEN, AND WHERE?

What dosage of medicine must I take?

What questions must I answer in the exam?

How do I get to the airport? What are the rules of the game?

How do I assemble this piece of furniture? How do I make chocolate chip cookies?

The ability to answer these kinds of questions depends on having an understanding of what instructions and direction are and how to translate them into actions. Understanding instructions involves both encoding—being able to give a command or a set of directions—as well as decoding—being able to translate what is meant by a command in order to carry it out or to follow a set of directives. Instructions can be given or received in many different ways, including auditory-verbal (e.g., directions given over the phone); written (e.g., a recipe in a magazine); visual (e.g., road signs or diagrams illustrating how to fix an appliance); audio-visual (e.g., an online training video); and even nonverbal (e.g., interpreting a parent's frown to mean "Not now!").

What Are the Thinking Skills Related to Instructions?

Instructions involve interpreting or giving a command, a message, or a set of directives or directions. Having a strategy helps with both encoding and decoding of instructions. A useful strategy is to ask the six *Wh* questions: *Who? What? Why? When? Which?* and *Where?* Applying answers, where appropriate, to these questions ensures that the correct sequence occurs in implementing the instructions. Errors in following instructions are also minimized if the right strategy and sequence is followed. When using the imperative statement in encoding instructions, care needs to be taken to ensure that the instruction or direction is clear and well presented. Different modalities can be used to suit different forms of instructions (e.g., a written recipe, a diagram to build a model, a verbal explanation for playing a game).

Why Are the Thinking Skills of Instructions Important?

There are many reasons for teaching the skill of giving and receiving instructions. The best way to illustrate the importance of being able to encode and decode instructions is to discuss the consequences of *not* giving or following instructions properly. For example, what are the consequences of a doctor not giving the correct instructions about dosage of medication? What are the consequences of not decoding (understanding) the essay topic on an exam? What are the consequences of not obeying the instructions of the road?

Giving and receiving instructions is an integral part of our everyday life—at school, at home, and in the community. Errors in following instructions can cause danger (e.g., not following the road signs), cause embarrassment (e.g., using salt instead of sugar in the baking recipe), or cause confusion (e.g., giving an incorrect date on a party invitation). Instructions require simultaneous use of a number of cognitive functions, including precision and accuracy in both input and output, as well as consideration of a number of sources of information, sequencing skills, and the ability to consider more than one source of information.

When and Where Are the Thinking skills of Instructions Used?

There are numerous contexts and situations were we give and receive instructions. In the home context, we are decoding and encoding from morning to night—from following the directions on the breakfast cereal box, to giving instructions to children about their chores, to operating the DVD in a set sequence at night. A typical day at school is controlled through giving and following instructions—for example, obeying the school rules, listening to the teacher's directions on how to conduct an experiment, and telling someone where and when to arrange transport. Our everyday lives are regulated by instructions such as how to install a software program, with whom to lodge a complaint, on what side of the road to drive, and so on. Giving and receiving instructions is a universal cognitive skill.

Cognitive Conundrum—Instructions

"Discoveries are often made by not following instructions, by going off the main road, by trying the untried" (Frank Tyger, n.d.).

Is there a case for *not* following instructions? Think of mediating challenge and a creative spirit in children. What do you think?

BRIDGING INSTRUCTIONS TO FORMAL LEARNING CONTEXTS

Numerous formal learning experiences can be used to mediate instructions.

Humanities

- Review the rules of spelling and grammar in a particular language (e.g., in English—*I* before *E* except after *C*).
- Observe the specific format, language, and layout of instructions in various institutions (e.g., finding a reference in a library, legal documents in councils).

Social Studies

- Discuss the protocols that everyone must follow during a session of Congress or during other governmental meetings (e.g., parliamentary procedure and decorum).
- Explore the rules and regulations that protect individuals in school or business environments.

Sciences

- Emphasize the importance of following specific instructions and safety precautions when conducting a scientific experiment.
- Show how dissection in the study of plants and animals involves following specific steps (e.g., in a flower dissection, starting from the sepals and working to the stigma).
- Demonstrate the importance of following mathematical rules and theorems (e.g., the order of computation when brackets are involved).

Arts

- Show why it is critical to follow the sequence of processes involved in silk-screening, making batik, developing photographs from film, and so on.
- Select a dance, such as the waltz or the Macarena, then write or diagram the set of instructions for that dance.
- Stress the importance of following the instructions or stage directions indicated in a drama script (e.g., move to center stage, exit back left).

Technology

- Show the step-by-step procedure that manufacturers need to follow in the making of a product from raw materials (e.g., refining sugar from sugar cane, extracting petrol from crude oil).
- Investigate the range of instructions given on software download and installation. Critically evaluate the user-friendliness of each.
- Review specific sets of rules and instructions that protect workers in their jobs (e.g., OHS—occupational health and safety procedures).

BRIDGING INSTRUCTIONS TO INFORMAL LEARNING CONTEXTS

General

- Carefully analyze assignment topics and instructions on tests and exams to ensure that you structure the answers as specified.
- Practice setting up and following directions (e.g., finding a specific place on a map, baking a cake, assembling a structure).
- Follow the rules of a game to avoid conflict and confusion.
- Explain the procedure for checking out books from the library.
- Read instructions for operating instruments or other appliances before using them.

Health and Personal Development

- Mediate "coping-with-life" strategies through following instructions (e.g., a pragmatic approach to using payphones and parking meters, reading schedules or timetables, filling in forms, interpreting traffic signs).

Home

- Show children how to build a model airplane by following the instructions systematically. Ensure all the correct airplane parts are used in the correct places and that they are assembled it in the correct order—otherwise, the finished product might be unsuccessful.
- Construct a tree house or playhouse from ready-cut pieces of timber. Follow instructions to make sure it is safe and correctly assembled.
- Practice following simple directions (e.g., growing plants from seedlings, following the rules of a game, operating and fixing new appliances, writing an invitation, taking telephone messages).

Creative

- Use the concept of *instructions* as a stimulus for creative, diverse, individualistic, and "reverse" thought, wherein sequence and laws of order are purposefully tampered with.
- Imagine the steps of your dad's favorite chocolate cake recipe have been mixed in the instructions pot. Pull out each step at random and follow your own recipe no matter what order it is in. What does the cake look like?

Multicultural

- Use the instructions instrument as a springboard to examine protocol and procedure in diverse cultures. Discuss and contrast rituals that various cultures practice, such as wedding ceremonies, baptisms (Christian tradition), bar mitzvah or bat mitzvah (Jewish tradition), quinceañera (Mexican tradition), prayer, spiritualism, and life instructions from a higher order or supreme being, and so on.

APPLICATION OF INSTRUCTIONS— IMPLIED INSTRUCTION

The skills involved in understanding instructions can be applied in the classroom setting. For example, consider the myriad of everyday signs and symbols where instructions are implied (e.g., "wheel chair only," "detour," "no parking," "loading zone"). Such nonverbal instructions, often implied, can be confusing for both children and adults.

There is a psychological and emotional component of instructions in which messages can be communicated and interpreted both verbally and nonverbally. Students need to be helped in their interpretation and response to such. We need to show them that instructions need not be written or announced. They can be conveyed through symbols, signs, gestures, paralinguistic cues, body stance, and even the juxtaposition of objects. Such cues may cause an emotional reaction—confusion, anxiety, and impulsivity. Aim to expose students to as many of these examples as possible and discuss them in terms of the consequences of misinterpretation.

FEUERSTEIN'S THEORY IN MEDIATING INSTRUCTIONS

Feuerstein's (1980) theory focuses on three areas that impact the development of the thinking skills. These include the *mediated learning experience* (MLE)—the type of interaction initiated by a mediator; the *cognitive functions*—the thinking skills of the learner; and the *cognitive map*—an analysis of the learning task. These three areas provide techniques for analyzing the interaction between the mediator, the learner, and the learning task. They provide a useful framework to use when mediating the thinking skill of *instructions.* This can be illustrated using the example of following a recipe.

Mediated Learning Experience

Feuerstein's (1980) criteria of MLE (see Appendix A) provide the mediator with techniques that help mediate the skill of instructions. In this example of following the instructions given in a recipe book, the mediator can instill in the learner the reciprocity needed to be able to focus on the task and decode the steps of the recipe (*mediating intentionality and reciprocity*). The mediator can then provide numerous examples of where following instructions accurately is important and necessary, thus eliciting the underlying concept of the task and bridging it to other examples in everyday life (*mediating transcendence*).

Cognitive Functions

The list of cognitive functions (see Appendix B) at the input, elaboration, and output phases give a framework for targeting specific skills needed to ensure the steps in a recipe are followed accurately and in the right sequence. For example, mediating questions such as "What is the next step?" and "What are all the ingredients needed?" will guard against impulsive data gathering (*precision and accuracy in data gathering and ability to consider more than once source of information at the input phase*). The sequence of steps can be checked off as they are completed and the different quantities of ingredients compared (*select relevant cues and spontaneous comparative behavior at the elaboration phase*). Finally, to avoid impulsivity in responding or trial-and-error responses, the mediator can model or talk through the process (*participatory and worked-through output phase*).

Cognitive Map

The cognitive map can be used to analyze and manipulate the learning task to ensure that it is pitched at a meaningful and useful level for the learner (see Appendix C). In this example, decoding a recipe is an everyday task (*content*) requiring skills in reading (*written modality*) and decoding the instructions to bake and cook successfully (*decreasing levels of abstraction, novelty, and complexity*).

Thus, the techniques of MLE, the cognitive functions, and cognitive map can be used to mediate the skill of decoding *instructions* by following a recipe.

WINDOW TO INTERNATIONAL
RESEARCH ON COGNITIVE EDUCATION

Instructions is the 10th instrument used in Feuerstein's (1980) Instrumental Enrichment (IE) program. Overall, there are 14 instruments that make up the IE program, which has been implemented in a range of contexts internationally. This extract describes research done using IE to bring about cognitive modifiability with severely disturbed clients:

> The findings by Skuy, Apter, and Dembo (1992) at the Geha Hospital in Israel, using Feuerstein's Learning Propensity Assessment Device, suggested that both those diagnosed as having a conduct disorder and those with schizophrenia were amenable to change and improvement of their cognitive deficits. A subsequent study by Hadas-Lidor (2001) at the same hospital considered the effectiveness of IE in rehabilitating clients with schizophrenia. For this study 58 schizophrenic, clients were matched equally into an experimental (IE) and a control group (treated with traditional occupational therapy methods). After one year, the results showed significantly differences between the IE and control groups on almost all the cognitive tests, and in particular for both memory and thought processes, as well as in work and residence status. There were no significant differences in the activities of daily living inventory or on a self-concept scale. The authors concluded that the successful outcome of their study points to the importance of including long-term cognitive intervention in rehabilitation of schizophrenic clients.

"How many a dispute could have been deflated into a single paragraph if the disputants dared to define their terms."

—Aristotle (384–322 BCE)

11

Progressions

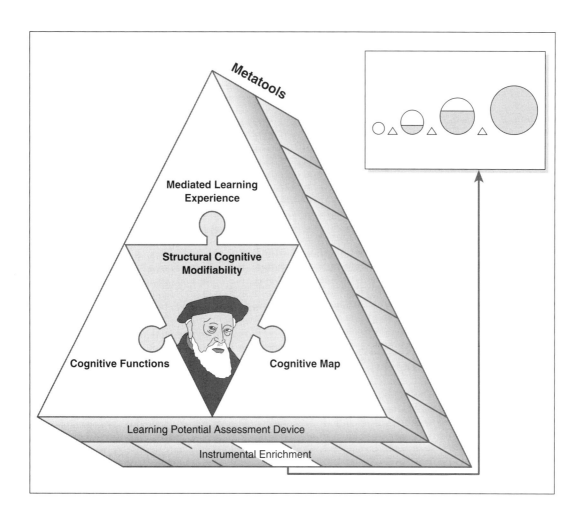

The thinking skill outlined in this chapter is *progressions*, which deals with the cognitive operations involved in looking for rules that govern the relationship between events. These rules are then applied in order to anticipate and predict new events. It focuses on identifying the relationships between events that cause them to be repeated in succession. For example, inducing the rule that thunder always follows lightning, and similarly deducing the event from the rule, that if I see lightning, I should hear thunder soon.

The thinking skill relating to progressions is taught in the *numerical progressions instrument*. Feuerstein's (1980) symbol for this instrument is a succession of circles and triangles. The rule that govern this particular progression is that a circle follows a triangle, the triangles stay the same, and the circles change in size and color. One can predict the possible continuation of this progression based on these rules.

PROGRESSIONS—WHAT, WHY, WHEN, AND WHERE?

> *If the color of the traffic light is now red, what color will it change to?*
>
> *In knitting a ribbed pattern for the sleeve of a garment, what follows a purl row?*
>
> *If the temperature drops below zero degrees, what will happen to water?*

Being able to answer these kinds of questions depends on having a good understanding of progressions. This means understanding that there are laws and rules that govern events, and that the future can be predicted based on knowledge of the past. It involves identifying the rhythmic succession of events. Understanding progressions overcomes the anxiety and insecurity that exists when events are considered to occur due to luck or chance or coincidence. This skill outlines how coincidence can be determined by examining the underlying relationship between two events. Some rules are stable and constant and result in the event always occurring (e.g., day follows night). Some rules are less stable and result in an event probably happening (an accident following drunk driving at excessive speeds); possibly happening (e.g., rain follows dark clouds) or happening occasionally (e.g., winning money following a lottery bet).

What Thinking Skills Are Related to Progressions?

Progressions are stable and recurring events in a sequence that are governed by a rule or formula. This can be likened to a pattern repeating itself according to a particular principle. When the rule or principle is determined, new situations can be anticipated based on that rule. Numerical progressions are an example of progressions that involve the modality of number—for example, 3, 6, 9, and 12 are a recurring set of numbers based on the rules of multiples of 3. Progressions can occur in all modalities and content areas (e.g., specific musical beats and rhythms, dance step sequences such as the waltz, poetry meter or refrain, applying mathematical and scientific formulae, patchwork quilt patterns).

Why Are the Thinking Skills of Progressions Important?

There are many reasons for teaching the skill of progressions. These include distinguishing between chance events (which are unpredictable) and causality (events that we can predict based on a rule or hypothesis generated from past occurrences). Being able to identify different types of progressions develops a deeper understanding of relationships, for example cyclical progressions—as in the seasons of the year—and linear progressions—as in the chapters, sections, and subsections of a book. Understanding progressions helps us appreciate ascending (adding on) and descending (subtracting) causal relationships, such as eating more calories than one burns results in weight gain (ascending progression), or spending more money than one earns results in bankruptcy (a descending progression). Finally, being able to distinguish between finite progressions (e.g., the life cycle of a moth) and infinite progressions (e.g., patterns of evolution) allows us to see how relationships can be subsets of each other.

When and Where Are the Thinking Skills of Progressions Used?

There are numerous contexts and situations were deducing and inducing progressions is needed. For example, induction is needed to discover the rules governing repeated patterns of behavior (e.g., in poetry and drama, that iambic pentameter involves five feet or beats in a line). Deduction is needed when we predict what will happen in the future based on the rules of a progression (e.g., working out the exponential growth in the population of the planet).

Cognitive Conundrum—Progressions

Does following a set of rules or constructs, which have been predetermined by past events and their outcomes, cause us to be inflexible in our future outlook and handling of situations ("a leopard can't change its spots")? What do you think?

BRIDGING PROGRESSIONS TO FORMAL LEARNING CONTEXTS

Numerous formal learning experiences can be used to mediate progressions.

Humanities

- Identify the rhyme, stanza length, and rhythm in various types of poetry, and then create a poem using these set rules.
- Observe the progressive themes used in film, playwriting, and other forms of storytelling (e.g., good winning over evil, happy endings).

Social Sciences

- Analyze and show how global events predict future outcomes based on past occurrences (e.g., spread of AIDS in Africa, use of sleeper cells in the spread of terrorism).
- Look at examples of how one can predict the effect of an accumulation of repeated occurrences (e.g., exposure to small amounts of radiation or asbestos can eventually result in cancer).
- Consider cycles in which events recur in the same sequence and according to the same rules (e.g., phases of the moon, months of the year, changes of tides, times of day).

Sciences

- Show how progressions occur in nature (e.g., water cycles, blood circulation, biorhythms, reproduction).
- Discuss natural rhythms of animals and "laws" of the jungle, which always pervade (e.g., birds migrating, fish spawning, mating cycles, survival of the fittest).
- Give examples of the applications of the laws of physics that result in natural progressions (e.g., solid to liquid to gas with an increase in temperature).
- Examine geometric and multiple progressions in mathematics and how they are represented graphically (e.g., ascending, descending, or linear graphs).

Arts

- Design and print repeated patterns for fabrics. Use overlays to produce new sets of patterns.
- Illustrate how an illusion of depth can be created in a drawing by using the rules of perspective.
- Study the continual rhythms of music and song to identify the underlying beat that holds the musical piece together.

Technology

- Demonstrate the need for constant monitoring of a progression. An error occurring in one phase of a production line can cause exponential harm all the way through the process.
- Construct set algorithms to design and test software used to predict outcomes that may or may not be favorable (e.g., movement of a typhoon over the ocean, an asteroid rushing towards earth).

BRIDGING PROGRESSIONS TO INFORMAL LEARNING CONTEXTS

General

- Explain how block scheduling of courses can be integrated so students know where to go and what books to pack on any given day.
- Show how the acquisition of skill and knowledge is a prerequisite for progression from one level or discipline to another.
- Play auditory memory games (e.g., "I went to the store and bought a . . ." in which each child repeats the progression and adds one item).

Health and Personal Development

- Encourage introspection of personal constants, rhythms, and progressions in development by reflecting on the past, present, and future (e.g., love has been a constant in my life, sadness has progressed to feeling happy and confident).
- Discuss the idea of being "master of one's own destiny" as a powerful tool in affective or emotional areas. Students can be empowered by being able to understand laws of the universe and how they affect personal choice.

Home

- Show how movement and music games can be played by building up a sequence of claps and steps based on a particularly rhythm (e.g., stand, crouch, cross your legs and up again—stand, crouch, cross your legs . . .).
- Design and knit a sweater by repeating certain stitches to create a particular design (e.g., a rib equals one purl stitch and one plain stitch repeated, and a stocking stitch equals one row plain and one row purl).
- Demonstrate rules in pattern work by designing and installing a mosaic or tile floor in the home.
- Generate rules to determine the daily routine in the home (e.g., wake up, make bed, eat breakfast, shower, do chores).

Counseling

- Demonstrate the need to look for connections between events to establish their cause and effect in order to handle future problems (e.g., what was the sequence or pattern of events leading up to a family feud).

APPLICATION OF PROGRESSIONS— CULTURAL CONSTANTS AND CONTINUITIES

The skills involved in the study of progressions can be applied in the community setting. For example, consider an event where a group of people, children or adults, from different cultural or ethnic groups share their ongoing traditions, customs, laws, and rituals with the rest of the community.

Laws, rhythms, cycles, and recurring phenomena have great value in different cultures. They are critical to the transmission and preservation of customs. In a society, it is important to celebrate the diversity and natural progression of rituals, customs, mores, and laws, which govern specific communities (e.g., family reunions every Thanksgiving, going to church every Sunday, having Shabbat meals every Friday night, fasting at Ramadan). Contrast annual cycles of Eastern and Western cultures based upon spiritual philosophies and religions. Consider the importance placed on rhythm in many of the Eastern ways of life for physical as well as mental endeavors (e.g., yoga, karate, mantras in meditation). We need to mediate to young people how these rituals can lead to stability, regulation, and continuity of culture and that they should be respected—whatever the culture.

FEUERSTEIN'S THEORY IN MEDIATING PROGRESSIONS

Feuerstein's (1980) theory focuses on three areas that impact the development of the thinking skills. These include the *mediated learning experience* (MLE)—the type of interaction initiated by a mediator; the *cognitive functions*—the thinking skills of the learner; and the *cognitive map*—an analysis of the learning task. These three areas provide techniques for analyzing the interaction between the mediator, the learner, and the learning task. They provide a useful framework to use when mediating the thinking skill of *progressions.* This can be illustrated using the example of predicting the next leap year.

Mediated Learning Experience

Feuerstein's (1980) criteria of MLE (see Appendix A) provide the mediator with techniques that help mediate the skill of instructions. In this example of predicting when the next leap year will be, the mediator will need to mediate the importance of working accurately at inducing the rule for the progression involved in a leap year (one every four years) and then deduce, using the rule, when exactly, without guessing or trial and error, the next series of leap years will be (*mediating self-regulation and control of behavior*). The mediator can then provide numerous examples of when rules need to be accurately induced and when events in a sequence can be predicted through deducing from the rule (*mediating transcendence*).

Cognitive Functions

The list of cognitive functions (see Appendix B) at the input, elaboration, and output phases give a framework for targeting specific skills needed to ensure that progressions are correctly identified and then predicted. Having a clear understanding of the verbal terms and sequences in time are essential for gathering data (*precision and accuracy in receptive verbal tools and temporal concepts at the input phase*). The ability to project the next event and give a justification for this is needed (*project virtual relations and provide logical evidence at the elaboration phase*), as are the skills of induction and deduction (*inferential and hypothetical thinking and hypothesis testing at the elaboration phase*). Finally, impulsivity in responding or trial-and-error responses need to be avoided (*precise and accurate data output*).

Cognitive Map

The cognitive map can be used to analyze and manipulate the learning task to ensure that it is pitched at a meaningful and useful level for the learner (see Appendix C). In this example, a numerical progression needs to be calculated (*content*) requiring skills in adding four years (*numerical modality*) and applying the rule to the example (*decreasing levels of abstraction, novelty, and complexity*).

Thus, the techniques of MLE, the cognitive functions, and cognitive map can be used to mediate the skill of *progressions* by calculating the next leap year.

WINDOW TO INTERNATIONAL RESEARCH ON COGNITIVE EDUCATION

Numerical Progressions is the 11th instrument used in Feuerstein's (1980) Instrumental Enrichment (IE) program. Overall, there are 14 instruments that make up the IE program, which has been implemented in a range of contexts internationally. This extract describes research done using IE with disadvantaged gifted adolescents in South Africa.

The effectiveness of IE for enhancing the cognitive and socioemotional functioning of disadvantaged adolescents in the Soweto Gifted Child Program in South Africa was investigated by Skuy, Mentis, Nkwe, and Arnott (1990). This was done over two years in a controlled study of 120 seventh- and eighth-grade students. The program was catered for gifted Black children from sociopolitically disadvantaged backgrounds, who were provided with extra academic instruction every Saturday morning. Students who followed the regular curriculum of the gifted program formed the control group, while matched samples of students were placed in two experimental groups: one that divided the available time between IE and the bridging of its principles to the curriculum, and another that, in addition, incorporated explicit components of creativity-enhancement and socioemotional development into the IE program. Significant improvements for both IE groups, relative to the control group, were found. Further, systematic bridging into the curriculum and explicitly addressing socioemotional factors and creativity improved the effectiveness with which tutors implemented IE in terms of the quality of mediated learning experience provided and the nature of teacher-student interaction.

"Whenever I want to understand what is happening today or try to decide what will happen tomorrow, I look back."

—Oliver Wendell Holmes Jr.

12

Transitive
Relations

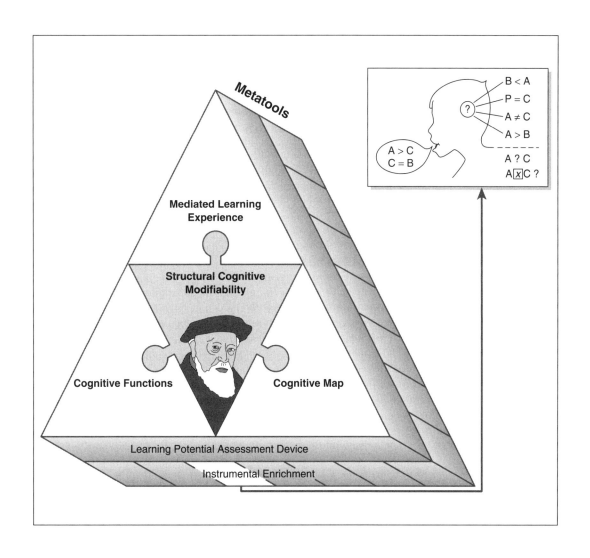

The thinking skill outlined in this chapter is that of *transitive relations*, which deals with the cognitive operations of transferring information we have from two pairs of items to a third pair. *Transitivity* is the property of transferring from one pair of terms to another. In transitive relations, we transfer from two premises, united by a middle term, to a conclusion. For example, Bill is taller than Rob, Rob is taller than Peter, and therefore Bill is taller than Pete.

The thinking skill relating to transitivity is taught in the *transitive relations instrument*. Feuerstein's (1980) symbol for this instrument is a person solving a problem that has been encoded in symbols. The person takes in information (B is less than A, B is equal to C, A is not equal to C, and A is greater than B); thinks through the problem (what is the relationship between A and C?); and, by transferring information, expresses the solution (A is greater than C, and C is equal to B).

TRANSITIVE RELATIONS—WHAT, WHY, WHEN, AND WHERE?

If Mark runs faster than Gina who runs faster than Sam, will Sam beat Mark in a race? How old is Jane if she is two years older than Mary and Mary is three years younger than Sue, who is 10? If car A is more expensive than car B, which is the same price as car C, do we know the price of car A?

Being able to answer these kinds of questions depends on being able to solve problems of transitive relations. This means finding the conclusion by transferring information from two premises. It involves using the common term in both statements (Gina is slower than Mark but faster than Sam) to reach a conclusion about a third statement (Mark is faster than Sam). In transitive relations, we look for relationships between elements to transfer to other relationships between elements.

What Are the Thinking Skills Related to Transitive Relations?

Transitive relations refers to the transitivity of relationships: If information is given about two statements, then a conclusion can be inferred about a third statement by transferring the relationship of the common term. For example, if we know the relationship between A and B and between B and C, then we can transfer the information to reach a conclusion about A and C. The transitive relations instrument uses the following symbols:

$>$ (greater than)

$<$ (less than)

$=$ (equal to)

$\neq$ (not equal to)

x (unknown)

? (unknown, as there is not enough information)

Working out whether an attribute of an item is greater than, less than, equal to, or not equal to the same attribute in or of another item, allows those items to be placed on a continuum according to that attribute. Placing items along the continuum enables relationships to be determined. Items can then be ranked—for example the relative strengths of a concentrate, the relative expense of houses, the relative value of different currencies, and so on.

Why Are the Thinking Skills of Transitive Relations Important?

There are many reasons for teaching the skill of determining transitive relations and where items are ranked. These include making inferences and drawing conclusions about relationships using information from other relationships. For example, if Marc is considered a better tennis player than Simon, and Simon is better than Paul, then we can infer or draw conclusions about the outcome of a tennis match between Marc and Paul. Transitive relations can also be used to test statements for their validity— so as not to jump to illogical conclusions. For example, if Sally and Sue did not have the same mother, but Sue and Mary did, then it is not logical to call Sally and Mary sisters. Transitive relations enable us to move from the concrete to abstract by solving problems with the use of symbols (>, <, *x*, =, ≠, ?).

When and Where Are the Thinking Skills of Transitive Relations Used?

There are numerous contexts and situations were transitive relations are used. Ranking, for example results in a finer description of the relationships between sets of items (e.g., ranking the quality of items parallels ranking their grade, value, or the cost of the item). Solving transitive relations equations can also provide support for whether inferences can be made from the information at hand or whether more information is needed (e.g., if we are given the cost of one brand as being more than another brand, we still do not have enough information to draw conclusions about a third brand).

Cognitive Conundrum—Transitive Relations

Are there times when looking for relationships, comparing, and ranking can be a negative practice?

For example, do standardized, norm-based tests, which rank highest to lowest, negatively affect some students who fall in the lower ranks and as a consequence have limited opportunities. In this example and others, is there a danger that we overlook other important criteria, but which are not related and therefore not included in the assessment of individuals. What do you think?

BRIDGING TRANSITIVE RELATIONS TO FORMAL LEARNING CONTEXTS

Numerous formal learning experiences can be used to mediate transitive relations.

Humanities

- Review the use and expression of comparative adjectives (e.g., *fine, finer, finest*).
- Develop vocabulary to describe characteristics of objects or a range of feelings through using a continuum of words (e.g., *joyful, happy, excited, elated*).

Social Sciences

- Analyze and rank nations in terms of key criteria (e.g., economic status, productivity, political power). Look for links and overlaps.
- Develop a realistic understanding of the perceptions and attitudes of politicians by discussing different points of view and ranking them from extreme to moderate.
- Examine statistics on geographic phenomena such as temperature over a period of time, and then indicate which areas are hotter than others, which suffer more droughts, which have higher rainfall, and so on.

Sciences

- Discuss ranking of elements in the periodic table in terms of relationships. For example, if hydrogen is less dense than oxygen, and oxygen is less dense than helium, then which is denser—hydrogen or helium?
- Use the >, <, and = signs to illustrate relationships (e.g., to illustrate a larger or smaller quantity or number of elements in a set and to determine the relationship between all elements).
- Show how a sudoku challenge can be solved by comparing various numbers in rows, columns, and grids then establishing relationships between these.

Arts

- Use color charts to grade and discuss the range of hues within a specific color band (e.g., reds).
- Show how singers are selected in a choir by ranking their voices in terms of pitch and amplitude—alto, tenor, soprano, counter-tenor, and so on. What are the musical relationships between them?

Technology

- Demonstrate how architects achieve balance in their designs by comparing and juxtaposing various structures (e.g., two towers linked by a low level walkway, use of graded archways to expand space).
- Assess new products and inventions by ranking them in order of key criteria, such as ease of use, energy saving, value for money, after sales service, and so on.

BRIDGING TRANSITIVE RELATIONS TO INFORMAL LEARNING CONTEXTS

General

- Rank reading books in order of difficulty by comparing language, text, style, content, and so on.
- Design a chart in order to match the level of skill of players in a tennis tournament.
- Arrange class members in height order for a class photograph.

Health and Personal Development

- Help alleviate exam stress by ranking study material in terms of volume and priority then drawing up a study timetable.
- Demonstrate how sports prowess is built by ranking skills in degrees of difficulty and working at mastering each level (e.g., dives from boards of different heights, ski run grades).

Home

- Settle family disputes by encouraging siblings to rank themselves according to age. Explain why older children get different privileges (e.g., Jennifer > Paul > Mary, therefore Jennifer goes to bed later than Paul and Mary).
- Explain to children that in order to solve a problem you need to consider all the relevant information. For example, Suzie is shorter than Dov. Angelo is three feet tall. How tall is Dov? Is it possible to solve this problem without having more information?
- Read labels on foodstuffs, and rank them according to fat or sugar content.
- Prioritize music for a party or disco (e.g., disco songs first).
- Rank household chores in an order of frequency and importance to ensure they are completed.

Community

- Demonstrate the importance of ranking community issues in order of their degree of urgency for resolutions. This, in turn, can help in the planning of future community projects.
- Use the idea of ranking to illustrate "weighing the alternatives." This idea is useful in the formulation of strategies to solve problems in business and the community, as it can save a great deal of time and expense.

Multicultural

- Mediate the idea of equality, inequality, and ranking, which has deep roots in various cultures. These concepts often form the basis of harmony and conflict in intercultural groups as well as within the particular mainstream or predominant culture.
- Contrast cultural groups in terms of what is considered equal or unequal, greater or less than, as in the following: males/females, young/old, polygamy/monogamy, federal law/religious law, public secular education/religious education.

APPLICATION OF TRANSITIVE RELATIONS— GLOBAL GREED

The skills involved in the study of transitive relations can be applied in the community setting. For example, consider the following on results of a large international corporation vying for rights to clear forestland for a new pulp mill.

Economic greed leads to deforestation and deforestation accelerates species extinction. It follows, therefore, that economic greed results in species extinction. Further, the greater the green house gas emission responsible for global warming, the greater the climate change as a result of increased global warming. Thus green house gas emissions are linked to climate change. These sets of relationships need to be considered by a community when businesses wish to expand (e.g., building a new pulp mill, planting new crops, building new farms, extracting oil or gas from the seabed, sinking new gold mines, uranium extraction). An understanding of how one element impacts on another can lead to more stringent legislation of business expansion and more well-considered planning. It is the responsibility of communities to promote action, which monitors global greed and protects the environment.

FEUERSTEIN'S THEORY IN MEDIATING TRANSITIVE RELATIONS

Feuerstein's (1980) theory focuses on three areas that impact the development of the thinking skills. These include the *mediated learning experience* (MLE)—the type of interaction initiated by a mediator; the *cognitive functions*—the thinking skills of the learner; and the *cognitive map*—an analysis of the learning task. These three areas provide techniques for analyzing the interaction between the mediator, the learner, and the learning task. They provide a useful framework to use when mediating the thinking skill of *transitive relations.* This can be illustrated using the example of ranking student according to age.

Mediated Learning Experience

Feuerstein's (1980) criteria of MLE (see Appendix A) provide the mediator with techniques that help mediate the skill of transitive relations. In this example of ranking students according to age, the mediator can show the importance of recognizing uniqueness and difference of all individuals when compared with others, that there fine distinctions to be made along a continuum of any particular attribute (*mediating individuation*). The mediator can provide an explanation of the purpose of engaging in this task (why ranking age is important for matching age-appropriate reading material, etc.) and bridge the underlying concept of ranking to other examples in everyday life (*mediating meaning and transcendence*).

Cognitive Functions

The list of cognitive functions (see Appendix B) at the input, elaboration, and output phases give a framework for targeting specific skills needed to ensure that the activity of ranking students is accurate and provides insight into the process of looking at concepts, such as older, younger, and equal-aged. For example, the age of each individual member needs to be documented (*clear exploration and ability to consider more than once source of information at the input phase*). The ages then need to be remembered and compared against the ages of other members (*broad and wide mental field and spontaneous comparative behavior at the elaboration phase*). Finally, the response needs to be well articulated and accurate (*participatory and worked-through responses and adequate expressive verbal tools in the output phase*).

Cognitive Map

The cognitive map can be used to analyze and manipulate the learning task to ensure that it is pitched at a meaningful and useful level for the learner (see Appendix C). In this example, the task requires ranking according to age (*content*) which involves skills in comparing years (*numerical modality*) and plotting ages along a continuum, which will get easier with practice (*decreasing levels of abstraction, novelty, and complexity*).

Thus the techniques of MLE, the cognitive functions, and cognitive map can be used to mediate the skill of *transitive relations* through this example of ranking according to age.

WINDOW TO INTERNATIONAL
RESEARCH ON COGNITIVE EDUCATION

Transitive Relations is the 12th instrument used in Feuerstein's (1980) Instrumental Enrichment (IE) program. Overall, there are 14 instruments that make up the IE program, which has been implemented in a range of contexts internationally. This extract describes research done using IE with Ethiopian immigrants in Israel.

A number of studies have shown the value of using IE with Ethiopian immigrants to Israel. Thus, for example, Kozulin and Lurie (1994) studied a group of new immigrant teachers from Ethiopia. Participants in the study received intensive IE intervention over 16 months for 352 hours, as part of their retraining and recertification as teachers in Israel. Their level of cognitive functioning was initially lower than would be expected. The authors attributed this to the focus on specific and narrow skills by the education system to which they had been exposed, and their lack of preparation for novel problem-solving tasks. IE produced highly significant improvements in the participants' cognitive performance as measured by performance on the Block Design and Raven's Matrices, tests of nonverbal reasoning. In another study (Kozulin, Kaufman, & Lurie, 1997), 700 new immigrant children from Ethiopia received IE as part of the program of summer day camps. Concurrently, their teachers and counselors received intervention regarding their interaction with the children. Results reflected both quantitative and qualitative gains in the children's performance on standardized tests.

"If someone is violent towards those who seek freedom, that's bad. But if those who seek freedom use violence to achieve it, that's good."

—Michelangelo Antonioni

13

Syllogisms

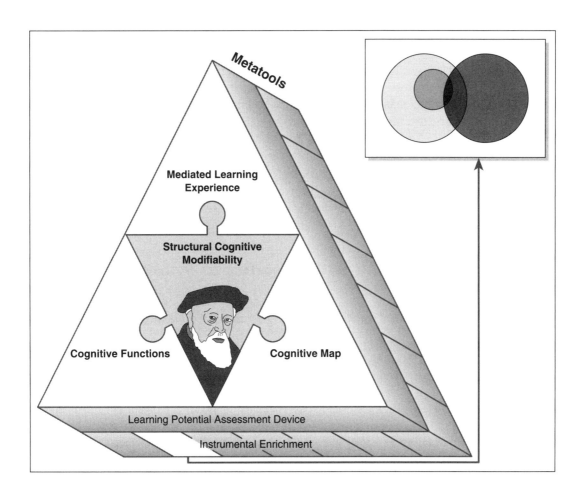

The thinking skill outlined in this chapter is that of *syllogisms,* which focuses on the cognitive operations involved in syllogistic reasoning, where from two given premises that have a common middle term, a third premise is deduced—called the conclusion. For example, "All men die, Socrates is a man, therefore Socrates will die."

The thinking skills relating to syllogistic reasoning involve understanding sets and set membership and are taught in the *syllogisms instrument* of Feuerstein's (1980) Instrument Enrichment (IE) program. Feuerstein's symbol for this instrument is a series of overlapping circles that represent sets. Some members belong to more than one set, which is indicated by a subset and intersecting sets. This instrument covers the areas of sets and set membership (e.g., a banana is a member of the set *fruit*) and the resultant reasoning that comes from analyzing set membership, called *syllogistic reasoning* (e.g., if all fruit is edible, and a banana is a member of the set *fruit*, then bananas are edible).

SYLLOGISMS—WHAT, WHY, WHEN, AND WHERE?

> *If the age restriction of a film is over twenty-one, can a ten-year-old attend?*
>
> *Is the statement "All accountants are introverts" true and logical?*

The ability to answer these kinds of questions depends on the ability to understand sets and subsets and to reason syllogistically. To answer the age-restriction question involves understanding mutually exclusive sets. The film is for all members of a set of people over twenty-one. If you belong to a set of people younger than twenty-one, then you are excluded from the rules governing the over–twenty-one set. Answering the second question about generalizations involves identifying sets and subsets. *Introvert* is a description of a subset of the universal set of accountants and thus cannot be used to describe the universal set, because there are some accountants who are not introverts.

What Are the Thinking Skills Related to Syllogisms?

Syllogisms are a form of reasoning based on an analysis of the relationships between sets and the members of sets. There are five underlying principles to analyzing sets and set membership that syllogisms are based on.

1. Identifying members of a set (e.g., Sally, Mary, and Sue are all members of set A, *females*)

2. Identifying mutually exclusive sets—where no member of set A is a member of set B (e.g., set A, *females* and set B, *males*, have no common members—no females are males)

3. Identifying identical sets—where all members of A are members of B, and all members of B are members of A (e.g., set A, *females* has the same members as set B, *girls*, where all females are girls, and all girls are females)

4. Identifying universal sets and subsets—where all members of B are also members of A, but only some members of A are members of B (e.g., set B, *mothers* is a subset of the universal set A, *females*, where all mothers are female but not all females are mothers)

5. Identifying intersecting sets—where some members of A are members of B, and some members of B are members of A (e.g., set A, *females* and set B, *teacher* are intersecting sets, where some females are teachers, and some teachers are females)

Syllogistic reasoning then stems from understanding the relationship between members of sets, subsets, intersecting sets, universal sets, exclusive sets, and identical sets. For example, if Sally is a teacher and some teachers are mothers, is Sally a mother?

Why Are the Thinking Skills of Syllogisms Important?

Syllogistic reasoning is important to understand and critically interpret statements made about the relationships between things in everyday life and to detect incorrect conclusions based on untrue statements. For example, the syllogism "All men are hostile, Adam is a man, therefore Adam is hostile" is logically valid but incorrect, because the first premise is a generalization that is untrue. So, from two related assumptions comes a conclusion that is logically valid but need not necessarily be true. As John Locke (1841) advised, "syllogism is thought to be of necessary use, even to the lovers of truth, to show them the fallacies that are often concealed in florid, witty or involved discourse" (p. 500).

When and Where Is the Thinking Skill of Syllogisms Used?

There are numerous contexts and situations were syllogisms are needed. For example, to interpret rules and regulations at home, at school, and in the community. For example, perhaps you want to know if you must wear your school uniform on a particular day; you could use the following syllogistic reasoning to determine the answer: "School uniforms are compulsory on weekdays; today is a weekday, therefore I must wear a school uniform." Syllogistic reasoning also shows the errors in laws—for example, a Senate Bill in the United States that stated, "All public acts of excretion are prohibited." Following syllogistic reasoning, if sweating is an act of excretion, sweating is not allowed in public! This error arises from overinclusion of membership in the set *excretion*. The set was defined too broadly to include sweating, which is an excretion, which was clearly not intended to be included in the prohibited public acts. Another example is the following billboard, which read, "A really nice home is hard to find. Oaks Homes are hard to find." The implication then, from syllogistic reasoning, is that Oaks Homes are really nice!

Cognitive Conundrum—Syllogisms

Structuring of faulty premises can lead to confusion, racial prejudice, stereotyping, and so on. Is there a danger that, without careful monitoring, encouraging children to always formulate sets of premises could lead to incomplete statements and illogical conclusions? Would it not be more prudent and less confusing for children if they were to work on single statements of fact? What do you think?

BRIDGING SYLLOGISMS TO FORMAL LEARNING CONTEXTS

Numerous formal learning experiences can be used to mediate syllogisms.

Humanities

- Analyze literature in terms of mutually exclusive sets according to the style or period in which the selection was written. Use premises to create the set.
- Appraise the language of logic and statement of premises used in various forms of literature and philosophy.

Social Sciences

- Identify the humor and absurdity in political or editorial cartoons by syllogistically analyzing the portrayal of a given situation.
- Arrange artifacts into mutually exclusive sets from different historical periods (e.g., the Stone Age, the Ancient Greeks, the Dark Ages).
- Explore the various subsets within the universal set of citizenship (in terms of origin, American citizens can be German, Dutch, Chinese, Mexican, etc.).

Sciences

- Explain how omnivores make up the intersecting set of herbivores and carnivores. Use premises and syllogistic thinking to test the placement of various animals.
- Use Venn diagrams to teach mathematical representations (e.g., universal sets, intersecting sets, empty sets, subsets).
- Generate different examples for identifying sets (e.g., all even numbers and all numbers divisible by two constitute identical sets). Use syllogism to test this (e.g., all even numbers are divisible by two, eight is an even number, therefore eight is divisible by two).

Arts

- Explain how an orchestra is made up of a number of subsets of various instruments that play together in unison. Identify the instruments that belong to a specific set (e.g., percussion, wind, brass, string).
- Appreciate different forms of dance by identifying the overlaps in steps, style, type of music, and so on (e.g., modern dance is a combination of jazz and other dance forms).

Technology

- Demonstrate the need for sets of logical premises in the writing of software algorithms for computer, machine, and robotic operations.
- Discuss the use of syllogistic thinking in the evaluation of technologies (e.g., this particle can accelerate to 500 meters per second; the sound barrier is broken at approximately 330 meters per second; therefore this particle breaks the sound barrier).

BRIDGING SYLLOGISMS TO INFORMAL LEARNING CONTEXTS

General

- Show how cognition can be seen as the intersecting set of all subjects as thinking skills are common to all disciplines.
- Draw a Venn diagram to illustrate class participation in common and unusual extramural activities.
- Use the principle of illogical verbal reasoning in the creative mode to illustrate the importance of valid versus invalid conclusions (e.g., all monkeys are hairy; my daddy is hairy; therefore, my daddy is a monkey!).

Health and Personal Development

- Use the overlapping sets theory in syllogisms to aid students in career choice (e.g., show how different professions have common elements—for instance, mathematical ability—and similar professions may call for different skills).
- Demonstrate the importance of formal propositional logic in overcoming prejudice, overgeneralizations, and stereotyping (e.g., all short people have inferiority complexes, all kids are naughty), that wrongly transfer the characteristics of the subset to the universal set.

Home

- Discourage stereotyping when assigning household chores (e.g., washing dishes and washing the car should not be exclusively boys' or girls' jobs).
- Talk about illogical syllogisms (e.g., all sweet things are good to eat; this is a sweet; therefore let me eat it!).
- Detect the "odd one out" by applying rules of membership of a set (for example, a hammer does not belong in a silverware drawer in the kitchen).
- Use intersecting sets to find common interests for family entertainment.
- Explain to young children that the family name is the common element in the intersecting set, but they retain their own identity in their first name (i.e., the first name, in a family, is an exclusive set).

Counseling

- Evaluate feelings relating to being a member of different sets. It is important in developing the socioemotional side of the student.
- Encourage students to analyze feelings that may be common to many social groups or unique to one specific group (e.g., *emos* focus on their emotional needs and the expression thereof).

Multicultural

- Review cultures in terms of their joint ownership of certain laws, customs, and rituals and, at the same time, identify their mutual exclusivity. For example, consider the belief in many Eastern cultures that the spirit proceeds to a higher plane after death, or consider various coming-of-age rituals, religious or otherwise, in different cultures.

APPLICATION OF SYLLOGISMS—SILLY SYLLOGISM

The skills involved in the study of syllogisms can be applied in the academic setting. For example, consider a group of children and/or adults formulating silly syllogisms to illustrate the dangers of drawing illogical conclusions.

Whilst syllogism can be used to formalize our use of logical statement, we do need to be aware of the dangers involved in the faulty logic that can arise in premises and deductions (e.g., Alzheimer's is a disease; Alzheimer's affects old people; therefore you will get Alzheimer's when you are old). This type of deduction is misleading and can result in prejudice, bias, generalization and other forms of faulty reasoning, all of which have negative outcomes in decision making and problem solving. We can mediate this faulty logic with children through the use of silly syllogisms (e.g., fish swim in water; fish need oxygen; we swim in water; we need oxygen; therefore we are fish!).

FEUERSTEIN'S THEORY IN MEDIATING SYLLOGISMS

Feuerstein's (1980) theory focuses on three areas that impact the development of the thinking skills. These include the *mediated learning experience* (MLE)—the type of interaction initiated by a mediator; the *cognitive functions*—the thinking skills of the learner; and the *cognitive map*—an analysis of the learning task. These three areas provide techniques for analyzing the interaction between the mediator, the learner, and the learning task. They provide a useful framework to use when mediating the thinking skill of *syllogistic reasoning.* This can be illustrated using the example of not being seduced by advertisements of products endorsed by celebrities.

Mediated Learning Experience

Feuerstein's (1980) criteria of MLE (see Appendix A) provide the mediator with techniques that help mediate the skill of syllogistic reasoning. In this example of not being seduced by advertisements, the mediator can focus on the intention and purpose of the advertisement and show, through syllogistic reasoning, how it might be illogical, invalid, or overinclusive to equate the product with the film star (*mediating meaning*). A variety of different advertisements can be analyzed to show overinclusive generalizations or associations between products and activities (*mediating transcendence*).

Cognitive Functions

The list of cognitive functions (see Appendix B) at the input, elaboration, and output phases give a framework for targeting specific skills needed to ensure that advertisements do not lure us into false reasoning. For example, in order not to be seduced by advertisements for products endorsed by famous people, one first has to make the link between the person and the product (*capacity to consider more than one source of information at the input phase*) and then identify the logical error that buying the product will lead automatically to being included in the same subset as the famous person (*inferential-hypothetical thinking at the elaboration phase*), so as not to buy impulsively or relate to the world from a one-sided point of view (*mature communication abilities at the output phase*).

Cognitive Map

The cognitive map can be used to analyze and manipulate the learning task to ensure that it is pitched at a meaningful and useful level for the learner (see Appendix C). In this example, the task requires syllogistic reasoning through set membership (*content*), which involves drawing Venn diagrams of sets and subsets (*figural modality*) and reasoning abstractly from these diagrams that being in a set of *using the product* does not automatically give one membership to the set of *celebrities* (*high levels of abstraction, novelty, and complexity*).

Thus the techniques of MLE, the cognitive functions, and cognitive map can be used to mediate the skill of syllogism through this example of reading advertisements.

WINDOW TO INTERNATIONAL
RESEARCH ON COGNITIVE EDUCATION

Syllogisms is the 13th instrument used in Feuerstein's (1980) Instrumental Enrichment (IE) program. Overall, there are 14 instruments that make up the IE program, which has been implemented in a range of contexts internationally. This extract describes research done using IE with children from different cultural groups in South Africa.

Skuy and others (1995) conducted a cross-cultural comparison of the effects of IE on children in a South African mining town. The study assessed the effectiveness of IE for primary school pupils, combined with concurrent provision to their teachers of training in mediated learning experience and of curriculum packages embodying and bridging IE concepts. The effectiveness of the programs for groups of African, mixed race, and White English-speaking and Afrikaans-speaking fifth-grade pupils in the segregated schools of a mining town was assessed. Postintervention improvements for all groups on cognitive measures were significant, with varying results on scholastic, creativity, and self-concept measures. For the African group, the improvements were significantly greater than for the others, which was to be expected in terms of their extent of educational deprivation under the apartheid regime. By providing the teachers with resource material, which embodied the cognitive operations underlying IE, the researchers guided the teachers towards a way of teaching in line with the approach of IE and mediated learning. These stimulus materials were similar to and an extension of the bridging examples presented in this book.

"All men are mortal, and no Gods are mortal, therefore no men are Gods."

—Aristotle (384–322 BCE)

14

Scaffolding

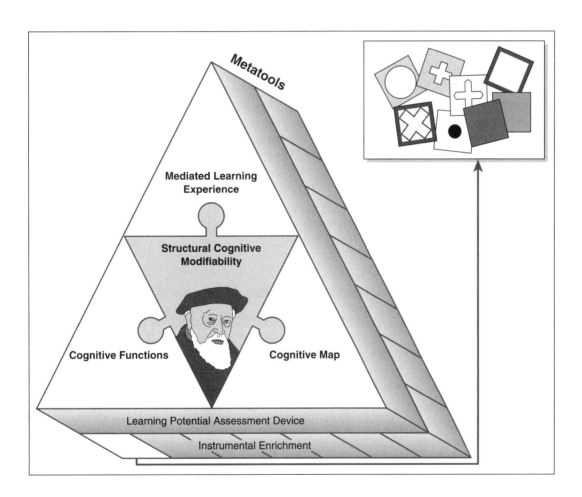

T he thinking skill outlined in this chapter is *scaffolding*, which focuses on the cognitive operations involved in mentally reconstructing an event or outcome by looking at the end product. It involves engaging at a metacognitive level to evaluate the cognitive skills used in a task. For example, reflecting on the formative feedback received on an assignment and applying this feedback to making the corrections needed for a better outcome.

The thinking skill relating to scaffolding is taught in the *representation stencil design instrument*. Feuerstein's (1980) symbol for this instrument is a series of templates of different shapes and colors that can be used to create a prescribed design when superimposed, on top of each other, in a particular order.

SCAFFOLDING—WHAT, WHY, WHEN, AND WHERE?

Why has this cake flopped? Where have I left my keys?

Who was the killer in the murder mystery, and how was the murder done?

The ability to answer these kinds of questions depends on the ability to reconstruct events in the sequence in which they occurred, with the help of available cues, and test out hypotheses against available evidence. One must mentally retrace one's steps to establish where the keys were left or go through the process of baking the cake to work out which part of the recipe went wrong. Solving a murder mystery means testing out different hypotheses one has against the available evidence. As new evidence comes to the fore, it changes our understanding of the previous information. Scaffolding involves mentally retracing which activities or events are used and in which order to create a particular outcome. This process involves discovering the meaning hidden in an event or discovering the motives underlying a particular action. For example, "acting out" or "disruptive" behavior in children could mask a cognitive dysfunction or be an inappropriate way of communicating a need or unhappiness. One would need to unravel the layers and look at available cues to test this hypothesis.

What Are the Thinking Skills Related to Scaffolding?

The skill of scaffolding involves a complex mix of a range of the cognitive skills previously taught. In order to reconstruct an event and reflect on an outcome, metacognition is required—that is, *thinking about thinking.* Thinking about thinking involves evaluating and acknowledging the role and function of the different cognitive operations, for example, the following cognitive operations—organization, which involves identifying unique characteristics of an event and how these fit within a structure; comparison, which involves identifying the similarities and differences between stimuli according to relevant criteria; categorization, which involves grouping according to principles; representational space, which involves orienting in space according to a referent; cardinal space, which involves orienting in space according to the cardinal points of the compass; analysis and synthesis, which involves reconstructing parts into a whole; problem solving, which involves identifying the disequilibrium in a situation; relationships, which involve identifying the connections and links within systems; time concepts, which involves sequencing and ordering events; instructions, which involves encoding and decoding rules; progressions, which highlight the sequences of events according to laws;

transitive relations, which involves ranking in order to infer relationships; syllogistic reasoning, which involves reasoning based on sets and membership of sets. These 13 thinking skills are all used in different ways and in different combinations within scaffolding—in deconstructing and reconstructing an event or activity.

Why Are the Thinking Skills of Scaffolding Important?

Scaffolding is an important thinking skill for a number of reasons. It is essential in appreciating that our senses can be tricked by illusions and that "seeing is not always believing" (e.g., the earth moves, not the sun). It also helps us distinguish between what we see and what we know (e.g., the earth looks flat, but when we reconstruct all the knowledge that we have about the earth, we know that it has to be round). Finally, scaffolding helps us unravel hidden meanings behind events (e.g., reconstructing a murder to solve the crime) and to look for hidden agendas (e.g., propaganda).

When and Where Are the Thinking Skills of Scaffolding Used?

There are numerous contexts and situations where reflecting metacognitively on a task is essential to move to higher order and abstract thinking and reasoning, for example, in the home (e.g., gaining insight into why the water in the swimming pool turned green); at school (e.g., gaining insight into the group dynamics of the class); in the community (e.g., understanding that some services were discontinued in order for others to be financed); to function creatively and efficiently (e.g., problem solving or looking for scientific reasoning).

Cognitive Conundrum—Scaffolding

Can the constant search for structures within structures, concealed meanings behind words, veiled messages, hidden agendas of individuals, and so on cause us to become cynical in our approach to life? Is a "nothing is as it seems" mentality constructive or destructive? What do you think?

BRIDGING SCAFFOLDING TO FORMAL LEARNING CONTEXTS

Numerous formal learning experiences can be used to mediate scaffolding.

Humanities

- Analyze poetry to identify the intention and appreciate the hidden meanings in the words.
- Review the use of language in delivering subtle or subliminal messages, particularly the "lingo" of subcultures such as emos (who stereotypically express dark and depressive *emo*tions), fluoros (who stereotypically wear bright, *fluo-rescent* colors), and Goths (who stereotypically wear *Gothic*, e.g., dominantly black dress, lipstick, and nail polish), and so on.

Social Sciences

- Facilitate understanding of events by considering historical perspectives and future implications (e.g., processes leading up to a coup d'etat).
- Decode meteorological charts to predict and report on weather conditions and their impact on populations, farming, and economies.

Sciences

- Mentally, retrace steps to determine what may have gone wrong in a science experiment, physics problem, mathematical computation, and so on.
- Research the possible causes of strange phenomena (e.g., asking, "Why do whales beach themselves?" "Why aren't the silkworms spinning?" "Why are the Tasmanian devils dying from tumors?").

Arts

- Explain the order and procedures used in making ceramics, pottery, batik, and other arts.
- Teach music appreciation by identifying overlap of various structures and instruments used to create harmony in a composition.

Technology

- Study the steps in a manufacturing process with particular reference to the order of operations and assembly. Mentally work out or visualize what the final product will look like.
- Study technological representations of, for instance, the path of a neurotransmitter, human DNA and gene placement, assembly of a nuclear warhead, plans for a new city, and so on. Show how these representative structures help us to better understand the unseen.

BRIDGING SCAFFOLDING TO INFORMAL LEARNING CONTEXTS

General

- Construct plans to facilitate changes in the management of an organization or school group.
- Consider factors in the environment that contribute to stress and devise strategies for minimizing them.

Health and Personal Development

- Individuals at risk need to be guided into identifying hidden dangers by looking for cues and projecting possible outcomes—ideally avoiding dangerous situations (e.g., a depressed child attending a party where there are drugs and underage drinking, a lonely adolescent communicating with a stranger on the Internet).

Home

- Teach children that some things exist even though they cannot be seen (e.g., explain that harmful germs and bacteria, although invisible to the naked eye, lead to tooth decay).
- Describe the steps followed in constructing a Lego or Brio tower or building (e.g., with Lego, start with a red, flat base block).
- Assist young children dressing for a special occasion by helping them decide which clothes they are going to wear and sorting out the order in which to put them on.
- Guide children toward understanding that there are a set of circumstances or reasons behind the behaviors of family members (e.g., "Brother is angry because . . .").

Community

- Illustrate the importance of looking at available clues to gain insight into problems (e.g., cancer clusters around microwave towers in the city).
- Use the idea of reconstructing or "looking back" to establish the specific order of circumstances that led up to an event in the community (e.g., strikes by a union of mine workers, a rapid increase of homeless people in a central business district).
- Extend the concept of mental reconstruction to the solving of crimes, looking for missing persons, examining the reasons for company mergers, and analyzing bull or bear runs in the stock market.

Multicultural

- Look for cues and clues to trace the manifestation of expressions, traditions, and customs in certain cultures, such as *the evil eye* from the Middle East, *saving face* from the Far East, *kowtowing* from China, *Day of the Dead* from Mexico, *Mardi Gras* from Western Europe, and so on.
- Explore behaviors in different cultures that deliver a "hidden message," which can be misconstrued. Consider the custom of burping loudly after a meal in the Middle East, as a compliment, that often misread by Westerners; or the averting of eyes in many cultures contradicts the Western importance of eye contact in communication.

APPLICATION OF SCAFFOLDING—PROJECT PLANNING

The skills involved in the study of scaffolding can be applied in the classroom setting. For example, consider a group of children working on a project where they need to plan and construct a model of a volcano from a photograph.

Students are often presented with a two-dimensional picture of a complete model, which they need to build and supply documentation for. Typical examples include the solar system, a volcano, a medieval village, and ecofriendly city. Without the thinking skills inherent in scaffolding, students can find the task difficult and usually engage parental help in the process. As teachers, we can use scaffolding to facilitate project planning (e.g., building a model of a volcano). For instance, we can use the deconstruction process to break down the elements depicted by the two-dimensional picture of a volcano. Consider those elements that may be hidden or implicit. Transfer these elements into a mental depiction of a three-dimensional model where cognizance of the order of construction is paramount. In mentally structuring the building process, students need to envisage the order in which they lay down the materials, glues, paints, chemicals, rocks, vegetation, and so on, to achieve the desired model.

FEUERSTEIN'S THEORY IN MEDIATING SCAFFOLDING

Feuerstein's (1980) theory focuses on three areas that impact the development of the thinking skills. These include the *mediated learning experience* (MLE)—the type of interaction initiated by a mediator; the *cognitive functions*—the thinking skills of the learner; and the *cognitive map*—an analysis of the learning task. These three areas provide techniques for analyzing the interaction between the mediator, the learner, and the learning task. They provide a useful framework to use when mediating the thinking skill of *scaffolding.* This can be illustrated using the example of understanding bullying in everyday life situations.

Mediated Learning Experience

Feuerstein's (1980) criteria of MLE (see Appendix A) provide the mediator with techniques that help mediate the skill of scaffolding. In this example of understanding bullying, the mediator can instill in the learner the belief that there is the potential for resolution and that perhaps through a restorative justice process both parties (bully and victim) can move to different ways of interaction (*mediating the search for an optimistic alternative*). The mediator can show them how in reflecting on the reasons behind the bullying, there is the opportunity for a different reality (*mediating self-change*).

Cognitive Functions

The list of cognitive functions (see Appendix B) at the input, elaboration, and output phases give a framework for targeting specific skills needed to ensure the steps in understanding and resolving bullying are effective. For example, clear communication of the different points of view of the situation are needed (*capacity to consider more than one source of information at the input phase*). The situation needs to be described carefully, the background behind the feelings and actions explored, and the context explained (*accurate definition of the problem; adequate elaboration of cognitive categories at the elaboration phase*). Finally, care needs to be taken to avoid emotional outbursts and blocking behavior as well as an egocentric or one-sided perspective of the situation (*mature, participatory, and worked-through output response at the output phase*).

Cognitive Map

The cognitive map can be used to analyze and manipulate the learning task to ensure that it is pitched at a meaningful and useful level for the learner (see Appendix C). In this example, the task requires participation in a restorative justice process to overcome bullying (*content*), which involves all parties presenting their views of the situation and listening to others (*verbal and auditory modality*) which might be challenging if unfamiliar (*high levels of abstraction, novelty, and complexity*).

Thus, the techniques of MLE, the cognitive functions, and cognitive map can be used to mediate the skill of scaffolding through this example of participating in restorative justice process.

WINDOW TO INTERNATIONAL
RESEARCH ON COGNITIVE EDUCATION

Representational Stencil Design is the 14th and final instrument used in Feuerstein's (1980) Instrumental Enrichment (IE) program. Overall, there are 14 instruments that make up the IE program which has been implemented in a range of contexts internationally. This extract describes research done using IE in Venezuela.

Sharron (1987) described a project conducted in Venezuela with the support of the government of that country as one of the boldest ventures ever undertaken in cognitive education. He noted the inclusion of certain thinking skills programs in the project, one of the chief of which was IE. A study that Sharron cites as emanating from this project assessed teachers' responses to IE. The study (conducted by Gonzalez, reported in Sharron, 1987) yielded inter alia the following findings: The attitudes of the teachers to the effectiveness of IE with their students were very positive. For example, 90% of teachers considered that IE had improved their students' analytical skills, while 63% said that there had been improvements in children's organization regarding school tasks; 90% of teachers considered their students' self-images improved. The majority of IE teachers reported that they had learnt new skills and techniques. When asked if they wished to continue with the program, 72.6% of IE teachers enthusiastically said they did.

"It is one of the commonest of mistakes to consider that the limit of our power of perception is also the limit of all there is to perceive."

—C. W. Leadbeater

Appendix A

12 Criteria of Mediated Learning Experience (MLE)

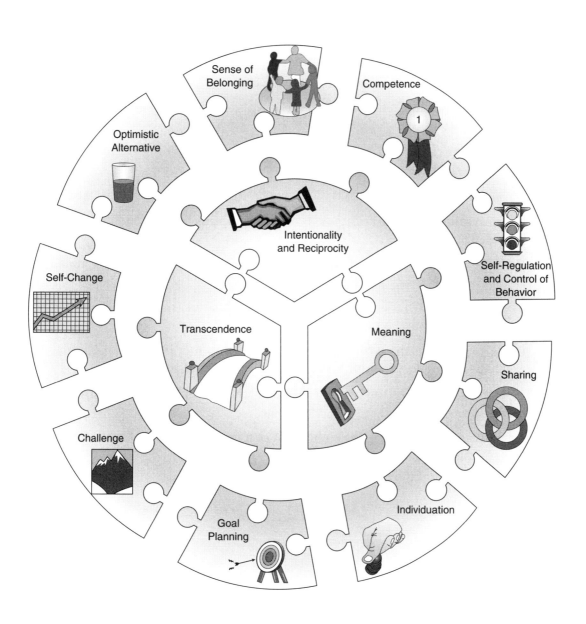

To date, Feuerstein has identified 12 criteria, or types of interaction, that are fundamental to mediation. He believes that the first 3 criteria are necessary and sufficient for an interaction to be considered mediation. The remaining 9 criteria may function at different times where and when appropriate and serve to balance and reinforce each other. Mediation is a dynamic and open process and should not be rigidly applied or fixed at just 12 criteria.

The 12 criteria of mediation include the following:

1. **Intentionality and Reciprocity** is a mutual interaction. The mediator has the intention to share, and the learner wants to receive.

2. **Meaning** occurs when the purpose of an activity is explained. It answers the learner's questions as to why the activity is important.

3. **Transcendence** is bridging from the immediate experience to underlying principles and related activities and ideas.

4. **Competence** means instilling in the learner a positive belief in his or her ability to succeed.

5. **Self-Regulation and Control of Behavior** involves "thinking about thinking" and adapting personal responses.

6. **Sharing** promotes sensitivity to others and emphasizes working together.

7. **Individuation** is the acknowledgment and appreciation of uniqueness and independence.

8. **Goal Planning** is the process whereby the learner is guided to set, plan, and achieve goals.

9. **Novelty and Challenge** is the feeling of excitement and determination when confronting a new and difficult task.

10. **Self-Change** is the recognition, acceptance, and monitoring of continual changes that occur within the learner over a period of time.

11. **Search for the Optimistic Alternative** is the desire for and belief in a positive outcome.

12. **Sense of Belonging** is the fulfillment of a need to be part of a group, family, culture, or community.

Appendix B

Cognitive Functions and Dysfunctions

Feuerstein has categorized the cognitive functions according to the three major phases of the mental act—namely, input, elaboration, and output. Although artificially separated into three phases, they don't necessarily occur separately in life. However, the subdivision is useful to analyze and describe thinking as well as determine what factors might negatively affect thinking. This model can be used by teachers and parents to better understand and help the child who is experiencing difficulties with a particular task.

For example, if a child fails in the task of classification, it is not enough to comment on the child's poor intelligence or inability to classify, but rather, the underlying causes of the difficulty, which can be found in one of the three phases of thinking, should be sought.

The inability to classify, for instance, may be due to underlying functions such as imprecise data gathering at the input phase, an inability to compare the items at the elaboration phase, or poor communication skills at the output phase.

A detailed analysis of a student's cognitive functions requires an in-depth understanding of the three phases of the mental act:

INPUT PHASE: TAKING IN INFORMATION (RECEPTION)

This is the phase in which information or data are gathered in order to solve a task. For example, it may involve efficient and accurate perception, adequate listening skills, solid understanding of the language and of the concepts of time, space, and quantity, as well as the ability to collect and examine many sources of information at one time.

ELABORATION PHASE: WORKING ON THE PROBLEM (PROCESSING)

This is the phase where the information or data are processed. Our minds work on the information we have gathered. For example, it may involve defining the task, comparing and integrating relevant sources of information, planning, hypothesizing, working through problems logically, and so on. This is the most important and central phase.

OUTPUT PHASE: COMMUNICATING A RESPONSE (EXPRESSION)

This is the phase where the information or data are communicated or presented.

Responses or answers to a problem are given. It involves accurate, appropriate, and efficient communication skills.

The following tables identify the cognitive functions and dysfunctions at each of these three phases.

Table B.1 **Input Phase of the Cognitive Functions**

Input	
Functions	*Dysfunctions*
Perception	
Clear	Blurred and Sweeping
Exploration of a Learning Situation	
Systematic	Impulsive
Receptive Verbal Tools and Concepts	
Precise and Accurate	Impaired
Understanding of Spatial Concepts	
Well-Developed	Impaired
Understanding of Temporal Concepts	
Well-Developed	Lack of or Impaired
Ability to Conserve Constancies	
Well-Developed	Impaired
Data Gathering	
Precise and Accurate	Impaired
Capacity to Consider More Than One Source of Information	
Well-Developed	Impaired

Table B.2   Elaboration Phase of the Cognitive Functions

Elaboration	
Functions	*Dysfunctions*
Definition of the Problem	
Accurate	Inaccurate
Select Relevant Cues	
Ability to	Inability to
Engage in Spontaneous Comparative Behavior	
Ability to	Inability to
Mental Field	
Broad and Wide	Narrow and Limited
Spontaneous Summative Behavior	
Need for	Lack of Need for
Project Virtual Relations	
Ability to	Inability to
Logical Evidence	
Need for	Lack of Need for
Internalize Events	
Ability to	Inability to
Inferential-Hypothetical Thinking	
Ability to Use	Impaired Ability to Use
Strategies for Hypothesis Testing	
Ability to Use	Impaired Ability to Use
Planning Behavior	
Need for	Lack of Need for
Elaboration of Cognitive Categories	
Adequate	Impaired
Grasp of Reality	
Meaningful	Episodic

Table B.3 Output Phase of the Cognitive Functions

Output	
Functions	*Dysfunctions*
Communication Modalities	
Mature	Egocentric
Output Responses	
Participatory	Blocking
Output Responses	
Worked-Through	Trial-And-Error
Expressive Verbal Tools	
Adequate	Impaired
Data Output	
Precise and Accurate	Impaired
Visual Transport	
Accurate	Impaired
Behavior	
Appropriate	Impulsive/Acting out

Appendix C

Cognitive Map

The cognitive map can be used as a tool for analyzing and manipulating a teaching experience to identify cognitive dysfunctions and improve thinking. It consists of four layers of analysis that can be unpacked to focus on specific aspects of the task. Each layer provides a different area of analysis and opportunity for interaction so that the task becomes a dynamic teaching, learning, and assessment tool. These four layers focus on

- the content or subject matter of the task;
- the modality or language of presentation of the task;
- the level of abstraction, novelty, and complexity of the task;
- the cognitive operation or thinking skills required by the task.

As the name suggests, the *cognitive map* offers a map whereby the teacher can navigate the learning situation to mediate cognitive functions.

Figure C.1 The Cognitive Map

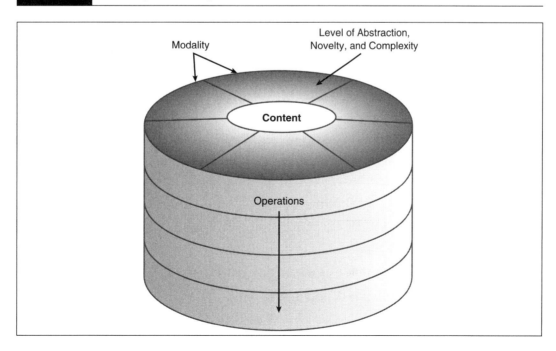

Glossary

abstract   ideas or concepts that are not concrete

affective   pertaining to emotions and feelings

analysis   separation of a whole into its component parts

autonomy   self-sufficiency and independence of the individual

bridging   transferring learned strategies and principles to other domains

categorization   to form objects, facts, subjects, or emotions, and so on into general class which predicates belonging

closure   completion

cognitive   pertaining to thinking skills or mental processes

comparison   juxtaposition to establish similarities and differences

concepts   ideas; general notions

cooperative learning   working together for mutual benefit

culture   a process by which knowledge, values, and beliefs are transmitted across generations

decentrate   the ability to see things from different perspectives

deduction   derivation of a conclusion by reasoning

disequilibrium   a state of imbalance; a problem

dysfunction   impaired or abnormal function

dysfunctional   impaired or disabled

empathy   understanding and identifying with another's feelings; putting oneself in another's shoes

empower   to develop an ability to act autonomously

episodic grasp of reality   the perception of reality as consisting of separate, isolated, and unrelated entities

external locus of control   attributing success or failure to outside forces; not taking responsibility for one's successes or failures

function   a specific task

hypothesis   a supposition made as a basis for reasoning

impulsivity   rushing into a task and acting without thought of the consequences

individuation the process of becoming a distinct entity

induction the process of reasoning from a part to a whole

infer to deduce or conclude from a variety of examples

intentionality to act by specific design

interaction the interconnection, interdependence, and movement among objects, events, ideas, or people

interiorization solving a problem in one's head

internal locus of control taking responsibility for one's own success or failure

intrinsic the basic nature of a person or thing

intrinsic motivation a desire to complete a task for its own value rather than for external rewards

instrument specific tool used to enhance cognition

instrumental enrichment Feuerstein's program to enhance cognition through mediation

lateral thinking problem solving in which the individual attempts to view the problem from many angles rather than to search for a direct, straightforward solution

logical evidence reasons available as proof to substantiate facts

manipulate to skillfully arrange objects, facts, subjects, or emotions

mediatee the person who receives mediation and interacts with the mediator

mediator an experienced and intentioned person, usually the parent or teacher, who interacts with the learner and interprets and explains the learning stimuli; the quality of this interaction will influence later learning or cognitive modifiability

mental act a stage of thinking

mental field the area of operating in one's mind

mental image a picture in one's mind

metacognition thinking about thinking; an awareness and understanding of one's thought processes and behavior

metalearning learning that goes beyond the basic fundaments

metatask a task designed to enhance metacognition

metathinking higher levels of processing thought

metatool specific instrument used to promote metacognition

modality the mode or manner in which something is expressed or communicated (e.g., MLE can be expressed in a number of modalities such as language, gesture, observation, etc.)

modeling demonstrating a type of behavior or action in order to illustrate something

modifiable having the potential to change

multiculturalism   the diversity of cultures

needs system   the internalized environmental demands that are made on an individual

operationalize   to show the application or use of

orientation   the act of changing position in response to an external stimulus

organization   to arrange or form into a coherent unity or functioning whole

peer tutoring   learning from fellow students

premise   a proposition supposed or proved as basis of an argument or inference

progression   sequence of numbers or events, which are continuous and connected by a law

reciprocity   equal return or counteraction

relation   connected by consanguinity or affinity

revisualize   to make visible in one's mind a distinct mental image

rote recall   the regurgitation of facts without necessarily understanding them

scaffolding   to construct mental platforms of structures, events, and so on

self-disclosure   expressing one's feelings and opinions

self-monitor   assessing and regulating one's behavior

set   a number of things of the same kind that belong together

stimuli   any objects, events, or ideas in the environment

summation   finding the total; giving a résumé

superordinate   outrank; superior in position

syllogism   a deductive scheme of formal argument consisting of a major and minor premise and a conclusion

synthesis   combining elements to form a whole

transcend   to rise above, surpass, span, go beyond

transitive   relating items such that if the first is related to the second, and the second is to the third, then the first is related to the third

Venn diagram   overlapping circles representing sets and subsets

virtual relationship   the essence of a relationship, rather than the actuality

visual transport   moving a mental image in one's mind

References and Suggested Readings

Ben-Hur. M. (2000, April). Feuerstein's instrumental enrichment: Better learning for better students. *New Horizons.* Retrieved January 2, 2009, from http://www.newhorizons.org/strategies/ie/hur.htm

Cooper, E. (2007). *Teaching for Intelligence.* Retrieved January 4, 2009, from http://www.nuatc.org/news/feuerstein.html

Feuerstein, R. (1979). *The dynamic assessment of retarded performers.* Baltimore: University Park Press.

Feuerstein, R. (1980). *Instrumental enrichment.* Baltimore: University Park Press.

Feuerstein, R. (1982). Learning to learn: MLE and IE. *Special Services in the Schools, 3*(1–2), 49–82.

Feuerstein, R. (1986). *L. P. A. D.: Learning potential assessment device manual.* Jerusalem: Hadassah-Wizo-Canada Research Institute.

Feuerstein, R., & Feuerstein, S. (1991). Mediated Learning Experience: A Theoretical Review. In R. Feuerstein, P. S. Klein, & A. J. Tannenbaum (Eds.), *Mediated learning experience (MLE): Theoretical, psychosocial and learning implications* (pp. 3–52). London: Freund.

Feuerstein, R., Feuerstein, R. S., Falik L., & Rand, Y. (2006). *Creating and enhancing cognitive modifiability: The Feuerstein instrumental enrichment program.* Jerusalem: ICELP.

Feuerstein, R., Hoffman, M., Jensen, M., Tzuriel, D., & Hoffman, D. (1986). Learning to learn: Mediated learning experiences and instrumental enrichment. *Special Services in the Schools, 3,* 48–82.

Feuerstein, R., & Jensen, M. (1980). Instrumental enrichment: Theoretical basis, goals and instruments. *Educational Forum, 44*(4), 401– 423.

Feuerstein, R., Rand, Y., & Hoffman, M. B. (1979). *The dynamic assessment of retarded performers: The learning potential assessment device, theory, instruments, and techniques.* Baltimore: University Park Press.

Feuerstein, R., Rand, Y., Hoffman, M., & Miller, R. (1980). *Instrumental Enrichment: An intervention program for cognitive modifiability.* Baltimore: University Park Press.

Feuerstein, R., Rand, Y., & Rynders, J. (1988). *Don't accept me as I am: Helping "retarded" people to excel.* New York: Plenum Press.

Gouzman, R. (1997). Major problems of blind learners using tactile graphic materials and how to overcome them with the help of the Braille FIE program. In A. Kozulin (Ed.), *The ontogeny of cognitive modifiability* (pp. 89–130). Jerusalem: ICELP.

Hadas-Lidor, N. (2001). Effectiveness of dynamic cognitive intervention in rehabilitation of clients with schizophrenia. *Clinical Rehabilitation, 15,* 349–359.

Keane, K. J. (1983). Application of mediated learning theory to a deaf population: A study in cognitive modifiability. *Dissertation Abstracts International, 44*(1–4). New York: Columbia University.

Kozulin, A., Kaufman, R., & Lurie, L. (1997). Evaluation of the cognitive intervention with immigrant students from Ethiopia. In A. Kozulin (Ed.), *The ontogeny of cognitive modifiability* (pp. 89–130). Jerusalem: ICELP.

Kozulin, A., & Lurie, L. (1994, July). *Psychological tools and mediated learning: Crosscultural aspects.* Paper presented at the 12th Congress of Cross-Cultural Psychology. Pamplona, Spain.

Locke, J. (1841). *An essay concerning human understanding.* UK: Oxford University Press. Retrieved January 13, 2009, from http://books.google.com/books?id=cjYIAAAAQAAJ& printsec=titlepage&source=gbs_summary_r&cad=0

Martin, D. (1993). Reasoning skills: A key to literacy for deaf learners. *American Annals of the Deaf, 138,* 82–86.

Mentis, M., Dunn-Bernstein, M., & Mentis, M. (2007). *Mediated learning: Teaching, tasks, and tools to unlock cognitive potential* (2nd ed.). Thousand Oaks, CA: Corwin.

Mulcahy, R., (1994). Cognitive Education Project. In M. Ben-Hur (Ed.), *On Feuerstein's instrumental enrichment: A collection* (pp. 129–144). Palatine, IL: IRI/Skylight.

Sanchez, P. (1991). A study of FIE as a tool for improving language proficiency. *Teaching Thinking and Problem Solving, 13,* 9–13.

Schnitzer, G., Andries, C., & Lebeer, J. (2007). Usefulness of cognitive intervention programs for socio emotional and behavioral difficulties. *Journal of Research in Special Educational Needs, 7,* 161–171.

Scottish Borders Councils School Project. (2005). *Life in the Borders: University of Strathclyde's evaluation of the Feuerstein pilot.* Retrieved January 2, 2009, from http://www .scotborders.gov.uk/life/educationandlearning/schools/20342.html

Sharron, H. (1987). *Changing children's minds: Feuerstein's revolution in the teaching of intelligence.* London: Souvenir Press.

Skuy M., Apter, A., & Dembo, Y. (1992). Cognitive modifiability of adolescents with schizophrenia. *The Journal of Child Psychology & Psychiatry, 33,* 583–590.

Skuy, M., Lomofsky, L., Green, L., & Fridjhon, P. (1993). Effectiveness of Instrumental Enrichment for pre-service teachers in a disadvantaged South African community. *International Journal of Cognitive Education and Mediated Learning, 2,* 92–108.

Skuy, M. S., Mentis, M., Durbach, F., Cockcroft, K., Fridjhon, P., & Mentis, M. (1995). Cross-cultural comparison of effects of instrumental enrichment on children in a South African mining town. *School Psychology International, 16,* 263–279.

Skuy, M., Mentis, M., Nkwe, I., & Arnott, A. (1990). Combining instrumental enrichment and creativity/socioemotional development for disadvantaged gifted adolescents in Soweto: Part 2. *International Journal of Cognitive Education and Mediated Learning, 1,* 93–102.

Thickpenny, J. P. (1982). *Teaching thinking skills to deaf adolescents.* Unpublished master's thesis, University of Auckland, New Zealand.

Tyger, F. (n.d.). *Creative quotations.* Retrieved January 13, 2009, from http://creativequotations .com/one/2452.htm

Webster's Revised Unabridged Dictionary. (n.d.). Retrieved January 11, 2009, from http://dictionary.reference.com/browse/synthesis

Williams, J. R., & Kopp, W. L. (1994). Implementation of instrumental enrichment & cognitive modifiability in the Taunton public schools: A model for systemic implementation in U.S. schools. In M. Ben-Hur (Ed.), *On Feuerstein's Instrumental Enrichment: A collection* (pp. 261–272). Palatine, IL: IRI/Skylight.

For further references regarding literature and resources in Feuerstein's Instrumental Enrichment, go to http://www.icelp.org (2008)

Index

CORWIN

A SAGE Company

The Corwin logo—a raven striding across an open book—represents the union of courage and learning. Corwin is committed to improving education for all learners by publishing books and other professional development resources for those serving the field of PreK–12 education. By providing practical, hands-on materials, Corwin continues to carry out the promise of its motto: **"Helping Educators Do Their Work Better."**